IDENTITY
OF
THE ADOLESCENT GIRL

IDENTITY OF THE ADOLESCENT GIRL

NEERJA SHARMA
Reader,
Deptt. of Child Development,
Lady Irwin College
(University of Delhi)
Delhi - (India)

DISCOVERY PUBLISHING HOUSE
NEW DELHI - 110002 (INDIA)

First Published - 1996
Reprinted-2011

ISBN 81-7141-347-1

Published by :

Discovery Publishing House
4831/24, Ansari Road, Darya Ganj,
New Delhi - 110 002 (INDIA)
Phone : 327 9245
Fax. : 91-11-3253475

Laser Typesetting by :

Debug Computer Services
Delhi.

Printed at:
Mehra Offset Press
Delhi

CONTENTS

Acknowledgements

It is with warm gratitude that I wish to thank Dr. S. Anandalakshmy, supervisor for this doctoral research, and former Director of Lady Irwin College, whose insightful hypotheses regarding growing up in India set the background for developing this study. Her consistency in provoking discussions during the course of the study helped shape the analysis out of a mass of descriptive data. Revising the thesis into a readable book was an enormous task. Once again, under the guidance of Dr. Anandalakshmy it became possible to complete it. I am very grateful to her for her contribution in reorganising the manuscript interestingly.

My friends and colleagues who extended to me logistic and moral support in the course of the study deserve my sincere appreciation. They are Ms. Bhanumathi Sharma, Dr. Nandita Chaudhary, Dr. Adarsh Sharma and Dr. Suniya Luthar.

I am indebted to all my subjects and their families for cooperating when the interviews were conducted in their homes and for extending hospitality during these visits. I am indeed grateful to two friends, one in Gurdaspur (Punjab) and one in Lucknow (U.P.), on whose worksites some young women in employment were interviewed without any loss of wages.

Special acknowledgements are due to the Headmistress, Ugoke Government High School, District Gurdaspur, and to the Headmistress, Sanatan Dharam Girls' Higher Secondary School, Patel Nagar, New Delhi, for granting permission to select subjects from their schools.

No words seem adequate to thank my family whose encouragement, support and involvement made it possible for me to complete this research project and the manuscript.

This research study was financially supported by the 3-year Teacher Fellowship granted by the University Grants Commission. The study was completed in 1983 and the degree was granted in 1985.

Neerja Sharma

Foreword

In the last decade the feminist discourse has generated a spurt of publications on women ; nevertheless, there is a dearth of material on the adolescent girl. This study was spurred by the need for informed views on that period, and there is no doubt that its publication will make a good contribution to the academic literature on female adolescence. In the combination of the quantitative data generated from a detailed questionnaire, with qualitative descriptions of the adolescent girl's perceptions of her status and options, new ground in broken.

Neerja Sharma has been innovative in including a review of selected contemporary literary work in Hindi and English in addition , of course, to the conventional review of published research available at the time of her study. This inclusion adds texture and colour to the review and enables the reader to share the insights which informed the planning of the study.

The author has taken Erik Erikson's epigenetic model for the developmental span as the framework. The focus is on the stage of adolescence as the girl child enters it. Erikson has mentioned the specific characteristics of adolescent identity. One of the important outcomes of this research is the query on the universality of the theory and the psychological sense in considering culture specificity.

The adolescent girl's life chances and experiences are examined in the continuum of tradition-modernity ; samples are drawn from Delhi, Punjab and UP's rural and urban areas and from three levels of socio-economic status.

Apart from the substantial quantum of data there are profiles of adolescent girls from each category. It enables the reader to open a window on the everyday life of the girl in different economic strata. We hear them articulate their problems many of which arise from gender discrimination within the family. We also see the link of socio-economic status to the opportunity structure, clearly indicating a gender-poverty interaction of the disadvantaged.

There is in this book an excellent discussion and analysis of the findings, concluding in a challenge to the belief that good theories have to be generated elsewhere. That the context makes a substantial difference to the applicability of theoretical constructs is established.

Students of Child Development, Psychology, Education and Social Work will find it eminently worthwhile to peruse this study and derive insights from it.

S. Anandalakshmy,
Consultant in Child
Development & Education,
Formerly, Director
Lady Irwin College, New Delhi

June 19, 1996

1

INTRODUCTION

In any society that is patriarchal in structure the male has a higher status than the female. It follows that the birth of a daughter is seen as a less joyous event than the birth of a son. In India, there is a confirmation for this attitude in both written and oral tradition : myths, folk-songs, folk tales and classical literature. These sources as well as documented studies (e.g. Cormack, 1961(b); Madan, 1965; Minturn & Hitchcock 1963) point to the marked preference for sons over daughters all over India. Exceptions have been there of course, but in general, reactions to a female birth have varied from fatalistic resignation to open denunciation as a curse. A common blessing for a young married woman is "May you have many sons!"

A surge of world-wide feminist movements in last few decades has brought into the limelight the strong prejudice against women, who, it must be realised, constitute approximately half of humanity. There have been academic and journalistic speculations on the etiology of the historical and contemporary bias of societies in favour of the male. Attempts have been made to analyze why the myth of female inferiority has persisted and why the world is predominantly male-dominated and male-oriented. Needless to say, no single explanation has been satisfactory.

There is an inadequacy in research on female childhood and adolescence. While some studies on socialisation have provided a world view of girlhood in India (Anandalakshmy, 1975; Madan, 1965; Minturn and Hitchcock, 1963, Ross, 1961) few have taken adolescent girls as the focus. Researchers have dealt with the subject of women's status, (Cormack, 1961(b); Jacobson and Wadley, 1977; Kapur, 1974, Khanna and Verghese, 1978) and some studies and reports, using a sociological approach, have considered factors such as modernization, employment, education and marriage in relation to women's status (Hate, 1969; Kapur, 1976; Ranade and Ramachandran, 1970; Sethi, 1976; YMCA of India, 1971). However, the emphasis in these studies or reports is on adult women rather than on girls.

Due to relative lack of research material on Indian adolescent girls, it was deemed appropriate to review some Indian literature (writings acknowledged to have literary value) for insights into a girl's process of growing up and her socio-cultural environment. These sources were generative of hypotheses that could be tested out in social science research.

Literary sources are treated here as significant for information on Indian girlhood. The work of some prominent Indian and Indo-Anglian writers provides details on girlhood. It must be noted that girls and women have figured less often than males as the central figures in fiction. This observation mirrors the social reality in which women have been relegated to the background.

The literature of any culture may, in general, be considered to reflect the prevailing conditions. The honest attempt of a sensitive writer to depict his own society often communicates as much information as an enthography. He has the freedom to depict his perceptions and to raise the most controversial issues in the garb of fiction. As a result, the characters and situations, though fictitious, have the force of real individuals and life-like circumstances. A writer has the insight which an academic researcher may lack or may be prevented from stating in the absence of systematically gathered empirical evidence.

There is a great deal of literature in every Indian language; however, the discussion here would be limited to fiction in English and Hindi by Indian writers. These vignettes are not meant to trace a historical profile but to add the colour and texture for a composite picture of an Indian girl. This, it was felt, would be useful for comparisons with the data collected. The work in the post independence period of a few writers in English and Hindi has been reviewed to compose the prevailing image of girlhood.

Girlhood in Indian Literature

Only those pieces of work have been selected that portray young female characters. Among those who have written in English are Mulk Raj Anand, Bhabani Bhattacharya, Kamala Markandaya, Anita Desai, Ruth Prawer Jhabwala and Rama Mehta. The modern Hindi writers whose writings have been selected are Amrita Pritam, Krishna Sobti and Nirmal Verma among others.

Reading over this literature the reader becomes conscious of the leitmotiv whether the story is set in the North (Punjab, Rajasthan), or the East (Assam, Bengal) or the South (Tamil Nadu). There is sorrow and anguish, sometimes loathing, that accompanies the birth of a daughter and a contrasting euphoria at the birth of a son. In Markandaya's *Nector in a Sieve* (1980), Rukmani is full of anticipation before her child is born. However, when she discovers that her child is a girl, tears of weakness and disappointment come, "For what woman wants a girl for the first born?" (P.14). Rukmani's husband Nathan also pays scant attention to the girl for the first few months because "He wanted a son to continue his line and walk beside him on the land, not a puling infant who would take with her a dowry and leave nothing but a memory behind" (P.15). The same couple is overjoyed when seven years later a son is born to them. Nathan's elation is obvious when he invites the whole village for a feast of rejoicing.

There is further evidence of distress over the birth of a daughter in Rama Mehta's *Inside the Haveli* (1977). Geeta, the daughter-in-law of the aristocratic family, whose story is depicted in the novel, and Lakshmi, a maid servant in the household, both give birth to daughters on the same stormy night. Lakshmi's husband presumes that the baby is a girl as he hears the child cry, even before the midwife announces this because "had it been a boy, Sarju (the midwife) would have come out.....shouting in her shrill voice, 'It is a boy, it is a boy, Give me money". However, since Geeta's daughter was the first grandchild of the *Haveli,* her birth was celebrated with pomp and show.

A feeling of distress overcomes Maya in Anita Desai's *Cry the Peacock* (1980) when she overhears a conversation between two women at a party that Mrs. Lal had four daughters. Maya cannot understand that feeling as her own father had always rejoiced in her saying "In a daughter he had a treasure"(P.71). Nevertheless, the thought of four daughters crowds her mind with vision of dowries, of debts, humiliations and burdens for the whole family.

In Amrita Pritam's *Pinjar** (1973) Pooro's mother, having had four daughters and a son, becomes pregnant again. She performs a series of rituals and religious offerings to invoke the gods for the birth of a son. The fact that a male child is born appears to strengthen the native belief in the power of such rituals in determining the sex of the child. In a short story *Ek Nishwas*,†also by Pritam, Viro's sister-in-law, speaking metaphorically, tells her that when a son is born the mother screams only once, but when a daughter is born she screams twice, once for the pain and the second time, for the sorrow.

The blessings on a bride or an expectant mother are always that she should have sons. Geeta in *Inside the Haveli* is always given the blessing "May you have eight sons" every time she touches the feet of the elders. The prejudice against the female is ingrained through the ceremonies surrounding marriage and prenatal rituals. For example, as part of the several marriage ceremonies in Punjab, when the bride comes to her husband's home, a baby boy is put in her lap, with a blessing that her first child be a son (Gill, 1977). In Gill's narrative of a family from Bhatinda (in Punjab) Preeto's sister-in-law, who has only a daughter, is an object of pity, or even fear, for she is considered to have the potential for casting the 'evil eye'. When Preeto gives birth to a boy there is the customary expression of joy; the midwife sings the song of congratulations and gets gifts in return. There are celebrations in all quarters and the mother (Preeto) is showered with gifts of clothes and jewellery.

Even when a would-be mother wishes to have a daughter as her first child, she has to keep her wish a secret, lest she be admonished by others for inappropriate thoughts. Mohini in *Music for Mohini* (Bhattacharya, 1952) is a young bride who is unaware of her mother-in-law's longing for a grandson. Then one day the mother-in-law hands her over a pile of old cotton cloth and coloured threads to make quilts

---

* A Hindi word meaning 'skeleton'.

† A Hindi phrase meaning 'a secret'.

for a child that may be forthcoming. A feeling of shame overcomes her as the mother pronounces, emphasizing the need for a son, "The family name will be carried for one more span of life on earth, and at the funeral anniversary of the departed, sacrificial water should be poured"(P.115). However, Mohini is puzzled with the emphasis on having a son, for she wanted to have a daughter. The mother-in-law's obsession for a grandson drives Mohini nearly mad. In agony she cries out, "I am needed only to bear a son.... Just as well I am barren....I won't have a son who is to be a limb of the cold, heartless Big House"(P.167).

In each of the above instances the reasons for the preference for sons are found in the age old customs of giving dowry at a girl's wedding and in the almost total breaking of contact with the girl once she is married. The son is seen as the ancestral link, since he continues the family name. He is perceived by the father as a support for his professional activities, and a redeemer of the soul from this world, as only the son can light the funeral pyre of his father. The mother of a son, whatever her status in the family hierarchy, can assert herself more than if she were the mother of a daughter.

Girls are often portrayed by writers as shy, obedient, and patient in their husband's presence. They do not flinch or retort even if the husband is being unjust. Once the girl is married, her parents also refuse to intervene in conjugal matters, for they believe that they do not have any right over a married daughter. In Pritam's *Pinjar* there is a poignant account of Taro, who is married to a man who already has a liaison with another woman. Taro suffers through the marriage and develop a psychosomatic illness; but her mother continues to exhort her to remain at her husband's house and to bear with the life ordained by Fate.

Bhattacharya's Mohini (1952), though an educated urban girl married in a village, combines the traditional traits of a modest bride with her education, talents and sensitivity. When married to Jayadev, also a learned young man, she prays only for his approval, having accepted him even before marrying him. Later, Jayadev tells her the story of his life, which she listens to with interests. But when she feels the need to tell him her own history, she is overcome with restraint. Jayadev does not seem interested in her past. This hurts her, but saying so is not a wife's prerogative.

In general, the traits of docility and self control in girls are appreciated as positive qualities. Mulk Raj Anand's Sohini (Untouchable, 1970) had "in her an inbred fortitude, obvious in her curious reserve, in her docile and peaceful bearing"(P.25). She is meek and composed in the face of her father's carpings at home and Gulabo's taunting at the well. Even when the priest at the temple molests her, she finds it difficult to relate the incident to her brother. Another one of Anand's characters is Leila in *Two Leaves and a Bud* (Undated). Although at an age when girls like dressing up she curbs her desire to buy trinkets in the bazar, realizing the poverty of the family. She helps her mother at home and with the plucking of the leaves on the plantation. When her mother dies, she takes over the running of the house, uncomplaining.

Bhattacharya's adolescent female characters are both comprising as well as bold. *In So Many Hungers* (1978), Rahoul, a city man, is flustered when Kajoli wants to wash his feet, a traditional practice in the village. The grandfather puts Rahoul at ease by saying, "She is a well bred peasant girl. She has a legacy of manners as old as India. How could she give up her manners and proprieties to suit your newfangled city ideas?" (P.28). But the same Kajoli, when almost forced into prostitution by famine and poverty, saves her honour through sheer will power and inner strength.

The second character that leaves an impact is that of Mohini (Bhattacharya,1952). Mohini has grown up exposed to the liberal ways of her father. He would take his children out for films and picnic in his car. She had read many romantic novels and formed romantic ideas about marriage. Her father gave her opportunities to express ideas about the suitors who came to meet her. Both of them had reacted sharply to the grandmother's approach to the issue of Mohini's marriage. Yet when the time comes and Mohini is married in a traditional village household, she moulds herself silently. Perhaps she remembers her grandmother's words of wisdom as she had left her home, "Honour your mother-in-law as though she were your mother,and abide by her will. Answer her hot words with absolute silence. Sweeten your speech when you talk to your neighbours. Words dipped in honey cost nothing. Bend yourself to the customs and traditions of the village"(P.66).

Rama Mehta's Geeta (1977) is also a city bred girl who has grown up in an environment of freedom. She has been educated at the

University where there is social interaction between men and women. When married to Ajay, the heir of an aristocratic family in Udaipur, she finds the atmosphere of the *haveli* conservative and oppressive. The total segregation of women from men during the day time and the formality that she has to observe at every step exasperate her. But she does not rebel openly. She remembers her mother's advice before her marriage, "Keep your head covered; never argue with your elders; respect your mother-in-law and do as she tells you. Don't talk too much"(P.14). Yet Geeta does not bend completely. Her pride prevents her from becoming timid like daughters-in-law in other *havelis.* At the same time, she does not give any opportunity to her overbearing mother-in-law to pinpoint any flaw in her conduct.

Internalizing parental injunctions and following instructions are traits that fit into the character of an Indian girl as two inseparable parts of an incomplete puzzle. This is seen in many novels and stories. *In Ganje Ki Kali* * by Pritam (1973), Gulbatti, who is a preadolescent, fancies playing a game with boys rather than with girls. But she remembers her mother who had warned her against playing with boys. The cultural restraint against mixing with the opposite sex has appeared quite vividly in the novel. Whenever a girl transgressed this role, harsh punishment was usually meted out to her. Maya in Anand's *The Village* (1954) is a playful, high spirited girl who enjoys playing with boys. Once when caught doing so her mother calls out sharply, "Maya *ni* Maya, eater of your husband, may you wither away! Have you no shame that you go sitting among men? You must learn to be shy and modest" (P.63).

The taboo against the girl's contact with any man other than her husband is shown to be very strong. In *Pinjar* (Pritam, 1973) Pooro is kidnapped by a Muslim lad from the family of Pooro's father's rival. Instead of protecting her when she escapes from her kidnapper, her family shuts the door in her face and beseeches her to go back to him as no one in their own caste would marry her after such an incident. Relating the story of a girl with a similar fate Krishna Sobti (1972) in her "*Dar Se Bichhudi*"† writes how Pasho becomes a pawn in the hands of circumstances. Because her mother, after she got widowed, had married a Muslim, Pasho is a victim of the taunting of her uncles, aunts and grand-

---

* Hindi name for Marijuana.

† A Hindi phrase meaning 'a bird separated from its flock'.

mother. In a desire to see her mother Pasho leaves her grandmother's house and goes to her mother. However, once she has moved out of a conventional role, she is ostracized by her family. When her husband dies in war, she loses status further.

Throughout the literature, whether Indo-Anglian or Hindi, girls get married in their adolescent years. In rural families the age at marriage is lower than in urban families. Gulbatti in *Ganje Ki Kali* (rural) is married off at 12 years. Pooro in *Pinjar* (rural) is to be married at 15 years. In *Nector in a Sieve* (rural) Rukmani marries off her daughter Ira at 15, while Preeto of Bhatinda (rural) is also wedded when she is 15 years old. Kajoli in *So Many Hungers* (rural) is about the same age when married. Among the urban girls Mohini is married at 17 years and Geeta (Inside the Haveli) at 19 years. Nimmi (Nature of Passion), Lekha (He who Rides a Tiger) and Sumita (Shadow from Ladakh) are not yet married at 18, 18 and 21 respectively.

The selection of the husband for the girl is almost always done by her parents, brothers or other close relations. Not only is the girl supposed to be ignorant about the transaction while it is being negotiated, she is also expected to accept the final decision and willingly marry whoever her family selects for her. A slight unwillingness or voicing of opinion in her own marriage is treated as violation of the code of modesty. If a girl ever decides to select her own marriage partner, she is at once labelled immoral even by her own parents. In *He Who Rides a Tiger* (Bhattacharya, 1955) there is a brief mention of a girl named Purnima who meets a young man Basav and is attracted towards him. Basav writes to Purnima's father making a proposal of marriage with Purnima. Both her parents are first stunned and then enraged. The mother beats up the girl cursing her for having being born at all. A few days later Purnima is married off to an old widower with grandchildren. This is her penalty for daring to make her own choice.

The education of the girl has been treated differently by different writers depending upon the eco-social setting of their characters. For instance, in Anand's *Two Leaves and a Bud* Leila, an adolescent girl, migrates from the heart of Punjab to the tea estates of Assam with her family. Having been brought up in poverty she has had no education. Pritam reveals the naivete of a village belle Anguri in her short story *Jungli Buti** (1973). Talking about the myth of evil effects of

* A Hindi term meaning "wild herb".

education for girls Anguri says that a village woman will sin if she gets educated. Reiterating the more pervasive view that educating the girl makes her headstrong and full of ideas is Taro's mother in *Pinjar.* She is exasparated due to her daughter's unwillingness to go back to her double crossing husband. The mother blames Taro's brother, who is educated, for sending Taro to school and making her bold.

A similar note is conveyed in Mehta's *Inside the Haveli* (1977). Geeta's mother-in-law is against sending Sita, a servant's daughter, to school as desired by Geeta. The older lady feels that "Once a girl has gone to school she will never take a broom in her hand". Sita continues to go to school on Geeta's initiative. Later when her marriage is fixed it is learnt that her in-laws want her to discontinue school once she is engaged to be married. One of the aunts in that family remarks, "It's enough for them to have a girl who can read and write. But a prospective daughter-in-law who is attending school would never be accepted by the elders and even the family would think she was lacking in modesty"(P.150).

Not always is the significance of literacy and education underrated. In Markandaya's *Nectar in a Sieve* Rukmani is proud of the little education which her father had imparted her informally at home saying, "For who knows what dowry there will be for you when you are ready!"(P.11). Rukmani keeps practising reading and writing so that she can teach her children when they are growing up. Kalo, who is a simple ironsmith in *He Who Rides a Tiger* (Bhattacharya, 1955) and has lost his wife in childbirth, aspires to send his daughter Lekha to an upper class private school. Lekha does extremely well throughout her schooling, bringing prizes and ranks every year.

Mohini (Bhattacharya, 1952) is also a motherless daughter and therefore, her father feels a special responsibility to look after her. Being a professor himself he sends Mohini for schooling against his own mother's wish, who prefers home training for her. *Shadow from Ladakh* is another one of Bhattacharya's (1966) novels that has a young educated girl Sumita as one of its main characters. Sumita's parents are Gandhian by belief and practice so that Sumita is brought up in a simple and ascetic environment. She uses her education to teach children of Gandhigram, the village where she lives.

Different from these cases is the portrayal of Nimmi by Jhabvala (1956) who belongs to a rich Punjabi business family in Delhi. For Nimmi, college education is a status symbol and going to college affords the opportunity to flaunt her expensive clothes, to cultivate friendship with girls from rich families, and to make friends with boys. On the other side are Nimmi's mother and *phuphiji* (father's sister) who vehemently disapprove of Nimmi being sent to college by her father. They regard college as a place where youngsters learn "Western ways" and unlearn the religious teaching of the home. *Phuphiji* thinks that at 18 Nimmi should be managing a household and bearing children, and not gallivanting about in a college.

There are cursory but sensitive references to the physical and emotional changes in girls at puberty sometimes from the girl's point of view and at other times from an outsider's perspective. In *Shadow from Ladakh*, Sumita's mother recalls the time when at 14, Sumita had come crying to her and had jabbed two fingers at her growing breasts, "I hate those,why must I have those?" When her mother had explained to her the laws of nature and the impending change in emotions, Sumita had hurtled back, "I don't want such feelings Mother" (P.308).

Markandaya (1973) has dealt with the subject of a growing girl's feelings and her perceptions of the adult world in her *Two Virgins*. While Saroja, who is not yet an adolescent, has childlike curiosity to know the subtle aspects of life, Lalitha, an adolescent behaves as though she is quite sure of what life is about. In one scene when both Saroja and Lalitha get drenched while bringing their buffalo back home in the rain, Lalitha peels off her clothes, runs out in the rain and shrieks with ecstasy. She flaunts her body with narcissistic pride in her sister's presence. The scene conveys very sensitively the feel of the effervescent moods and exciting sensations of an adolescent girl.

There is the case of Waddi, Rano's daughter, in Bedi's *I Take This Woman* (1967), who is just past puberty. "Waddi was like a jungle flower which bursts into full bloom with wild abandon"(P.28). Her mother, out of fear of miscreants in the village purposely dresses Waddi in rags and does not comb her hair. However, that does not prevent Waddi's innocence and good looks from making her comely and attractive. The surge of youth in the girl has been treated as a signal to find a match for her, lest she become a prisoner of her own new feelings and take some untoward step.

A particular relationship that has received attention in many novels is the father-daughter relationship. In the novels including *Shadow from Ladakh*, *Music for Mohini*, *He Who Rides a Tiger*, *Two Leaves and a Bud*, *Cry, the Peacock* and *Nature of Passion*, the father and the daughter have a special feeling for each other. Specially in stories where the girls have no mothers, the father is shown to draw emotionally close to his daughter as she grows up.

The mother daughter closeness is also depicted but with less emphasis. Fleeting instances of this are seen in Sobti's *Dar Se Bichhudi* when Pasho meets her mother for the first time in her life, and when in *Pinjar* (Pritam) Pooro is reminded through the marriage folk songs that she is to be married soon. Pooro embraces her mother crying. In general the girls are not seen to share their personal problems of growing up with their mothers. The mothers also seem not concerned to inform them about the impending changes that come with puberty. An exception is the case of Sumita's mother in *Shadow from Ladakh* who is an enlightened person and prepares Sumita for the physical and emotional changes she would go through after menarche.

A little removed from novels that describe the day to day events in the lives of their characters are a few that dwell on the imagination and deeper emotions of their young heroines. These are Anita Desai's *Cry, the Peacok* (1980), Krishna Sobti's *Blossoms in Darkness* (1979), and *Lal Teen Ki Chhat* by Nirmal Verma (1974). Maya and Rati, who are at the centre of the first two novels, carry the shadow of their past that blemishes their present also. Both of them, though now adult, have been through childhood experiences that have plunged them into a self imposed loneliness. In the third novel, Kaya is an adolescent girl who feels melancholic in her hilly surroundings and weaves a network of fantasy aroûnd her daily experiences.

The identity of a girl as it emerges through these pages of literature is that of a gentle, responsible, hardworking and self effacing person, encircled by constraints and expectations. Her individual traits become inconspicuous under the influence of social limitations and taboos. The level of education is low, as is the age at marriage. She treads the path of life paved for her by her parents, her husband and the countless traditional customs. She is cheerful in the face of hardships and intrepid when confronted with challenges.

Lack of Evidence on the Female in Theory and Research

The Indian social science community is not alone in neglecting the study of girls. Disregard of the female as a subject for academic concern is reflected in most of the classical theories in Psychology. For instance, traditional psychoanalytic theory does not take into account the destiny of woman. Freud simply made slight modifications of his account of the psychology of the male to explain that of the female. He explained feminine psychology in deficit terms rather than as a difference wherein all girls are aware of their low status. The absence of the penis in the female was held by Freud as the major cause for what he referred to as "female masochism".* It was suggested that every woman is masochistic and wants to suffer. Doubtless the exceptions were considered perverse females!

Erik Erikson, while postulating the eight stages of the human life cycle, kept both males and females in mind. An overview of his analysis of the crisis of identity of youth indicates that he did not feel the need to distinguish between the crises of male and female adolescent. His discussion, however, is with reference to a particular culture (the North American Middle Class) where, although male and female roles become polarized by the end of adolescence, the maturing girl has the freedom to "venture into 'outer space' with a bearing and a curiosity which often appears hermaphroditic if not outright 'masculine' "(Erikson, 1968, P.282) . In other words, it appears that there is a marked similarity in the nature and outlet of the conflicts and confusions of male and female adolescent in that culture, the issues leading to such upheavals being sex-appropriate.

---

* In traditional psychoanalytic theory the specific female functions and fantasies have been seen as primarily masochistic in nature. It maintains that early sexual wishes and fantasies concerning the father reflect the desire to be castrated by him. Menstruation is seen as a mutilative experience. Intercourse by the woman is said to satisfy her desire to be raped and violated and thus humiliated. Childbirth, in as much it is an antecedent of motherhood, has been considered a masochistic desire (Horney, 1973).

This view of childhood and youth cannot, however, be accepted as universally valid. Cultural influences are known to result in such differential socialization of children that sex differences are bound to become apparent at an early age. Thus people of a culture that prescribes totally different mores for male and female children, cannot be expected to view their adolescents with equivalence.

There was a fresh spurt on the scene of the Indian study of psychology when Sudhir Kakar proposed a psychoanalytic profile of childhood and society in India (1978). As a psychoanalyst he presented an impressionistic view of Indian girlhood based on a combination of his clinical experience, and anthropological and mythological accounts. On feminine identity he maintains that in the Indian society a woman's "identity is wholly defined by her relationship to others". He holds that over her life span the female is seen first as a daughter to her parents, then as a wife to her husband and lastly as a mother to her sons (and daughters). Kakar speculates that although there is cultural devaluation of the girl in this strongly male dominated society the girl derives her identity from her relationships with the other female relatives within her own family. In his words, "getting along with other women in this sphere, learning the mandatory skills of householding, cooking and childcare, establishing her place in the primary world: these relationships and these tasks constitute the dailiness of girlhood in India" (P.61).

Kakar's analysis of womanhood is insightful to understand North Indian upper caste families. However, his evidence is more mythological than clinical and therefore somewhat romanticized. It does not provide a model that takes into account variations in identity contingent upon developmental, social and cultural variables.

Adelson (1979), who is an author of many books on American adolescence, had admitted that "our knowledge of female development is virtually non existent" and that "adolescent psychology... is essentially the psychology of adolescent boys" (P.33). In the history of the study of adolescents there has been no parallel to the study of the male adolescent done by Offer (1969). Maccoby and Jacklin (1975) have reviewed research findings in the area of psychology of sex differences. While they found over 1400 published studies concerning sex differences in young boys and girls, they cited only 16 studies dealing with adolescent female development.

Pointing out research problems in the study of female adolescents, Benedeck (1979) remarked that, "ordinarily the male serves as the experimental subject, with the exception of studies which deal with sexuality and issues related to sexuality"(P.14). However, this has not hindered researchers from making generalizations regarding adolescence *per se*, defending this practice by the argument that concepts about males can be extended to females. There seems to be a male bias in the written material on adolescence, as in most of the research in psychology. Almost invariably, any discussion of parent child relationships is really a treatise on parent-son or rather mother-son relationship, the parent-daughter interaction being subsumed under the same discussion.

According to Singh (1975), studies on women and children have tended to receive secondary status in India because male researchers, who do not have access to female spheres of activity in a highly sex segregated society such as India, tend to ignore topics related with women and young children. In a male oriented set up such subjects are then given up as less important and hence perceived even by women researchers, competing with male colleagues, as detrimental to professional growth. This myth receives further impetus when women researchers, due to cultural constraints, are not able to mix as freely with male subjects as with females. They then tend to select field projects which require contact with women and young children. The danger of this tendency, as pointed out by Singh, is that studies on women reflect only the female point of view, that too specifically of those women who have themselves moved away from tradition in taking up professional careers. No social research can be totally value free. Every researcher brings to his/her piece of research certain biases that perhaps initially evoked his or her interest in the subject. Just as research on women that reflects only the "masculist" viewpoint has been criticised, similarly the same research which gives only the female view may be lacking in completeness.

Indian Studies on Socialisation

An academic approach to the study of girls as well as of sex differences in socialization is found in some Master's degree dissertations that deal with socially relevant issues using small samples. Preadolescents of both sexes from three different religious groups were studied to determine whether there was any relationship between independence training and the children's attitude to achievement (Bawa, 1972, Mathai, 1972; Saraf, 1972). In eight studies conducted on different communities to investigate the patterns of socialisation for competence, marked sex differences in socialisation practices were reported (Bajaj, 1973; George, 1973; Gill, 1974, Murthy, 1974; Sahai, 1974, Vasudev, 1974, Vohra, 1973, Yardi, 1972). Commenting on these studies in her paper, Anandalakshmy (!975) noted that the differences between the male and female roles were so marked that any measures of competence was not fair to girls since girls were assigned the less important jobs.

In a sensitive study of upper middle class adolescents (Menon, 1976) it was reported that both boys and girls perceived their pubescence as a period of gradual change, both physical and social. They viewed biological maturity as part of a continuous process; upheld parental values; and reflected orientations of obedience, deference and strong sex-role typing. Sex-role stereotypes of 13 and 16 year old adolescents were studied by Sareen (1981) and Makhija (1981) respectively. While both boys and girls were found to have stereotyped perceptions of the male and the female roles, in the former study boys emerged as more conservative than girls on sex-role stereotyping.

Focussing on the significance of the peer group in adolescence, urban girls' peer status has been studied in relation to their self concept and interaction with parents (Binepal, 1980; Gulati, 1980; Kumar 1980; Islam, 1976). No clear pattern emerged. However one finding that stood out was that among girls, interaction with peers did not override interaction within the family. The family continued to dominate most decisions well into adolescence. In another study of middle class adolescent girls (Khosla, 1982), the self concept was studied in relation to peer status and neuroticism as measured by the Neuroticism Scale Score. Peer ratings were obtained on the self esteem scale, peer acceptance, dissonance of self concept and N.S.Q. It was found that the girls who had low acceptance from peers or were seen by them as having low self esteem, and those who scored the highest on neuroticism had one characteristic in common. These girls had disturbed relationships with their parents. They had negative perceptions of their own family life, expressed dissatisfaction with parental attitudes and preferred to be left alone.

Some more recent studies on adolescent girls through Master's level research have been conducted by Bajaj (1990), Dhingra (1988),

Gupta (1988), Gill (1987), Nischal (1987) and Tandon (1988). Tandon's study in particular portrays the profile of adolescent girls in Delhi slums.

A relatively recent publication titled Growing Up in Rural India : Problems and Needs of Adolescent Girls (Kumari et al, 1990) has quite effectively brought into focus the status of the rural adolescent girl in India. It is a socio-demographic analysis based on a sample of 400 girls between 10 and 16 years, drawn from rural parts of Delhi, Rajasthan and Uttar Pradesh. The issues explored were education, marriage, work pattern and leisure, health status, wishes and aspirations, and problems faced by the girls.

The findings have shown that the educational levels of the girls are low, only 7.5 per cent being educated upto higher secondary. Early marriage is prevalent, as 21.75 per cent girls in the sample were already married before 10 years of age. The study found that all the girls were actively involved in housework ranging from cooking for the family to cleaning utensils, cleaning the house, washing clothes, sibling care, and care of cattle and fetching fodder. More than 50 per cent girls were out to fetch water. On the basis of their analysis of the needs and problems of the subjects the authors maintain that the adolescent girls had a very low self-image. According to them "this was due to the fact that they were always made to believe that their bodies are impure after puberty and that girls are weak and inferior, and are always object of attraction for males"(P.113).

A landmark study on the girl child was completed in 1994 under the auspices of the Department of Women and Child Development, Ministry of Human Resource Development, Govt. of India (Anandalakshmy, 1994). It was an action research study on 13,200 girls and their families, the age group of the girls being 7 to 18 years. The data were collected through 22 Women's Studies Centres of the University Grants Commission in 14 States of India. One of the objectives of the study was to assess the status of girls within the family in order to predict the position of women in the 21st century.

The findings on socialisation of the girls revealed that the birth of a girl child was desired and celebrated only by 2% of the families. The report observed, "If there is one cultural trait that cuts across barriers of religion, region and caste, it is this devaluation of the girl child" (P.227).

The Construct of Adolescence

There is a basic question to be answered at this juncture that has a bearing on the issue under discussion. Has the period of adolescence been recognized universally as having the same meaning? The emergence of the construct of adolescence as a distinct period of human development has a history that dates far back into history.* The concept of adolescence, as it is commonly understood in contemporary psychology, was first presented by G. Stanley Hall in 1904. It is believed that the notion was "on the whole an American discovery" (Demos and Demos, cited in Bakan, 1975, P.15). Hall's contention was that it was a period of "storm and stress" and that physical growth was "saltatory" during this period. For several decades after this view was propounded, researchers continued to "confirm" that adolescent years were marked with near pathological disturbances, non conformity, defiance of authority, struggle for emancipation, and the like.

Since psychological theories originated in Western cultures, their universality was first questioned by anthropological research. Margaret Mead (1939) challenged the concept of turmoil in adolescence on the basis of her observations of girls in Samoa, a South Pacific island. Emphasizing the role of cultural influences on personality development, Mead reported :

> The adolescent girl in Samoa differed from her sister who had not reached puberty in one chief respect, that in the older girl certain bodily changes were present which were absent in the younger girl. There were no great differences to set off the group passing through adolescence from the group which would become adolescent in two years or the group which had become adolescent two years before (P.196).

In 1969, a study by Westley and Elkin attempted to explode the prevailing notion of the adolescent period as being one of storm and stress. They found the upper class adolescent subjects to be fairly high on harmony and social adjustment by conventional standards. Working on the same lines, Bandura and Walters (cited in Bandura, 1975) studied middle class boys and arrived at findings quite contrary to the belief about adolescence. Their subjects perceived their parents as supportive and guiding, and maintaining close ties with them. The peer group

---

* In a collection of ancient Basholi paintings there is mention of the stage of adolescence. According to the author (Randhwa, 1959), Bhanu Datta, Who has written *Rasamanjari*, has classified sviya (who loves only her husband) into three categories according to age and experience : Mugdha (youthful and inexperienced), Madhya (the adolescent), and Pragalbha (the mature).

seemed to reinforce rather than defy the parental norms and standards of behaviour.

Departing from the usual pattern of studies, Konopka (1976) conducted a sensitive study of adolescent girls in the U.S.A. She interviewed nearly 1,000 girls in the age group 12 through 18 years, from various economic strata, and belonging to urban, suburban, small town and rural areas of 11 states. The results were classified under eight main headings : life goals, sexuality, adults, friends-loneliness, drugs and alcohol, school, youth organisations, and social-political concerns. Despite a fairly large sample, the author stressed that her study did not claim to "present a composite picture of the American girl" (P.7). Recognizing the tremendous differences among human beings at all ages, Konopka maintains that even though some similarities among the subjects as well as small subgroups were found, no generalisations would apply to all girls.

Erikson's theory of human development, that proposed a distinct stage of adolescence in the life cycle (1968), has greatly influenced theorizing about adolescent development. As can be seen in his Epigenetic Chart (Figure 1), the period of adolescence corresponds to the fifth developmental stage i.e., the stage of identity versus identity confusion. Like all other stages in his scheme, adolescence is related to the other stages that precede and follow it. The critical challenge to the individual during this period is the achievement of an "inner identity". Failure to come to grips with his inner self is likely to lead to a state of identity confusion in the adolescent. Erikson further stipulates that before a stable sense of identity is achieved, the individual must go through and resolve successive psychosocial crises. Thus, the development of a sense of identity in contrast to identity diffusion are believed to represent the polarities of the adolescent stage.

Erikson views adolescence as a "natural" period of uprootedness in human life. Drawing a parallel between an adolescent and a trapeze artiste he conceptualizes the young persons as being in the middle of a vigorous motion, who "must let go of his safe hold on childhood and reach out for a firm grasp on adulthood, depending for a breathless interval on a relatedness between the past and the future, and on the reliability of those he must let go of, and those who will 'receive' him" (1975(b), P.219).

VIII								Integrity versus Despair
VII							Generativity versus Stagnation	
VI						Intimacy v ersus Isolation		
V	Temporal Perspective versus Time Confusion	Self-Certainty versus Time Consciousness	Role Experimentation versus Role Fixation	Apprenticeship versus Work Paralysis	Identity versus Identity Confusion	Sexual Polarization versus Bisexual Confusion	Leader-and Followership versus Authority Confusion	Ideological Commitment versus Confusion of Values
IV				Industry versus Inferiority	Task Identification versus Sense of Futility			
III			Initiative versus Guilt		Anticipation of Roles versus Role Inhibition			
II		Autonomy versus Shame Doubt			Will to be Oneself versus Self Doubt			
I	Trust versus Mistrust				Mutual Recognition versus Autistic Isolation			

Fig. 1. Erikson's Epigenetic Chart (From Erikh, Erikson, Identity, Youth and Crisis, New York : Norton, 1968.)

The theory states that the adolescent boy or girl experiences a virtual revolution - physical, physiological and cognitive, within himself. While coping with these changes, he must also consider how he is going to deal with the varied intellectual, social, and vocational demands of adulthood. The delicate balance achieved by the individual at the end of the latency period is disturbed because of the process of genital maturation. With regard to his selfsameness and wholeness, so essential for a sense of identity, he is in a state of doubt, although only transiently. The very rapidity of the changes increases the difficulty of achieving and maintaining a perception of the self as clearly defined and consistent, both internally and over time.

As a result of these disturbances there is a developmental crisis, termed the "identity crisis" by Erikson. The adolescent's previous trust in his body and his control over its functions are suddenly shaken, and must be regained gradually by reassessing himself. He seeks a new identity which would recognise his psychosexual drives but at the same time be approved of by his peers. In a culture that provides many choices, he is in a state of vacillation - which one must be finally adopt? Identification with an ego-ideal or person no longer serves its full purpose. The adolescent must now make a gradual but full integration of all previous identifications, and thereby achieve an ego identity. But if the resulting self-definition becomes either difficult or proves inadequate, a sense of role confusion occurs, i.e. the crisis deepens. In such a case, the adolescent may solve his dilemma by adopting the identity of a delinquent, for instance, in preference to remaining a non entity.

The term identity has received special focus in Erikson's discussions about adolescence. According to him, "Identity includes, but is more than, the sum of all the successive identifications of those earlier years when the child wanted to be, and often was forced to become like the people he depended on" (1968, P.87). More simply, he states that, "An optimal sense of identity is experienced merely as a sense of psychosocial well-being. Its most obvious concomitants are a feeling of being at home in one's body, a sense of 'knowing where one is going', and an inner assuredness of anticipated recognition from those who count" (P.165). Erikson prefers to use the term *ego identity*, which he differentiates from the concept of *personal identity*. According to him a personal identity is based on "the perception of the selfsameness and continuity of one's existence in time and space and the perception of the fact that others recognise one's sameness and continuity". Ego identity for him means more than the mere *fact* of existence. Thus it refers to "the awareness of the fact that there is a selfsameness and continuity to the ego's synthesizing methods, the style of one's individuality" (1968, P.50)

The term crisis has been used by Erikson in a developmental sense "to connote not a threat of catastrophe, but a turning point, a crucial period of increased vulnerability and heightened potential" (1968 P.96). It refers to a period of struggle or active questioning in choosing among meaningful alternatives. Hence, the adolescent crisis is considered normative by Erikson; i.e. a normal phase of increased conflict characterised by seeming fluctuation in ego-strength as well as by a high growth potential.

The concept that the identity crisis is normative has been fervently endorsed in the Western countries to the extent that the absence of such a crisis is seen as a deviation. Erikson himself became aware of the fact that "identity crisis was a welcome concept not (or not only) because it made developmental sense as a transitional stage ... but because it helped to glorify the drama of youth, with all its dangers, as a semipermanent state quite desirable on its own terms" (!975(a), P.115).

An overview of literature on adolescence reveals that the identity crisis has been extolled beyond common sense. Conger (1977) is of the view that there is a tendency, particularly among clinicians dealing with upper middle class elite youth, to consider a period of acute identity confusion and turmoil as typical. Its absence is seen as almost automatically indicative of impending emotional disturbance. It is possible that some theorists have tended to exaggerate the intensity and the frequency of identity crisis among youth in general, and that in some cases they have misinterpreted the psychological significance of the absence of serious adolescent turmoil.

By virtue of its very definition, the term "crisis" presupposes the existence of a number of choices. Conversely, the absence of meaningful alternatives should rule out the possibility of crisis. In a relatively simple, static, preliterate society where identification models are few and compatible, role opportunities extremely limited and expectations clearly defined, the process of identity achievement may be a relatively simple task. In contrast, in a complex, rapidly changing, fragmented society, finding a true identity may become a cumbersome task for many. Questions that come to the fore at this juncture are whether the identity crisis in an inseparable experience of life, and whether it occurs most often during adolescence and not before or after.

The doubt arises as Erikson firmly states, "it must be realised, then, that only a firm sense of inner identity (supposedly achieved after a phase of symbolic turmoil) marks the end of the adolescent process and is a condition for further and truly individual maturation" (1968,. P.88). In other words, to be a mature adult, every individual should have been through the experience of adolescence, and by the same token, should have shared the crisis of that stage, viz., a state of role confusion, presence of near neurotic conflicts, lack of commitment and inter generational divergence.

Erikson maintains that the phenomenon of the "identity crisis" at adolescence was not discovered by him; rather that he had merely given the most obvious name to something that everybody had been through at one time, most probably at adolescence. Further, Erikson concedes that "under certain personal and cultural conditions developmental crisis can occur precociously". Therefore the identity crisis may also occur well before the onset of adolescence (1975(b)). A result of a forward shift in critical experiences can be a premature crystallisation of identity, which, in turn, is seen as an interruption in the process of identity formation (Douvan and Adelson, 1966). The danger, according to these psychologists, is a premature fixing of one's self image, which thereby limits one's capacity for continued self-definition.

Despite popular acceptance, the Eriksonian model of identity formation has been criticised as being a masculine one (Gallatin, cited in Benedek, 1979; Gilligan, 1982). It has been pointed out that the conflicts noted by Erikson in his theory have reference to the issues which men must work out in order to confront their adulthood - what vocational plans to formulate, what roles to play, what identity to assume, etc. To answer the question whether women can have an identity of their own before they know whom they will marry, Erikson stated that "much of a young woman's identity is already defined in her kind of attractiveness and in the selective nature of her search for the man (or men) by whom she wishes to be sought" (1968, P.283). In other words, he sees a woman's identity contingent upon the presence of men and their attitude to her.

Erikson's chart of the human life cycle is described by Gilligan (1982) as being defined by the male experience. Gallatin (Cited in Benedek, 1979) too pointed out that the conflicts noted by Erikson in his theory have reference to the issues which men must work out in order to confront their adulthood.

Erikson's approach to the study of identity formation considers the role of the individual only within a specific socio-cultural environment. A whole corpus of his writings attests the importance he has attached to both somatic and social factors in identity formation. Erikson holds that while a sense of identity means a sense of being at one with oneself in the midst of change, it means "at the same time, a sense of affinity with a community's sense of being at one with its future as well as its history - or mythology" (!975{a}, P.27). He contends that historical processes in society enter the core of personality in childhood. That is, past history remains with him in the form of the prototypes that guide the parental imagery, customary fairly tales and folk lore, superstition and verbal instructions to children. In the same way, he argues that, contemporary social models are both clinically and theoretically relevant. He believes that "the whole interplay between the psychological and the social, the developmental and the historical, for which identity formation is of prototypal significance, could be conceptualized only as *psychosocial relativeity* (1968, P.23). Evidently identity formation cannot simply be a developmental issue when we are constantly being confronted the world over, with questions related social, national, cultural, social class and professional identity.

That the process of identity formation may be extended beyond youth is also recognized (Conger, 1977). In technologically developed and in developing societies, the gap between early school life and the person's final acquisition of specialized work skills and role seems to be increasing progressively. The stage of "adolescing" has become a marked and sufficiently extended period; an accepted way of life between childhood and adulthood. Erikson has viewed it as a "psychosocial moratorium", since society sanctions a delay of adult commitments and permits role experientation to its members during this "bridge" period.

In sum, Erikson's theory of adolescent development states that every individual is destined to go through a period of active struggle to achieve a sense of identity, the period most likely being the years after puberty until the end of youth. In general, it is granted that the crisis can shift forward or backward under personal or cultural circumstances.

The Adolescent's Search for Identity

Several studies of identity have based their theoretical formulations on Erikson's model of identity development and have confirmed that the identity crisis is the inevitable psychosocial aspect of "adolescing" (Bronson, 1959; Constantinople, 1975; Marcia 1975; Marcia and Friedman, 1975; Waterman and Waterman, 1975). The construct of ego identity has been studied in relation to several other variables such as adjustment (Carpenter, 1975), morality (Podd, 1972) and psychological effectiveness (Rasmussen, 1964). These studies have employed standardized instruments to assess the variables under study and have used statistically appropriate methods of data analysis. However the attempt in each of them has been to distinguish the various stages of identity formation rather than to focus on the process by which it develops. The findings seem to fit Erikson's model of adolescent identity quite satisfactorily. A review of such literature gives the reader the impression that, notwithstanding individual differences, adolescents grow up in a predictable manner and that individual variations in personality configurations are less significant than patterns of similar and shared behaviours.

Thus there is support as well as challenge for the hypothesis that adolescence is a difficult period in development, both biologically and psychosocially. The latter type of studies tend to derive their formulations on the basis of cross cultural data. In some cultures adult status is granted to boys and girls going through initiation rites at puberty. Though these ceremonies mark the transition from childhood to adolescence or adulthood rather abruptly, the status of the individual is clearly confirmed. In other words, a social identity is conferred on the person. Cultural themes and socialization norms of a society are significant in determining whether its adolescents would reach adulthood without going through an identity crisis. It is not implied, of course, that pubertal vicissitudes in a biological sense are not recognized. How a particular culture deals with the inevitable biological changes is important because the interplay between pubertal development and the societal attitude will determine the psychological meaning of puberty for its members.

The theories and studies on adolescence seem to point to several common themes and assumptions which are as follows :

> The onset of puberty marks the beginning of adolescence. There are individual as well as cultural differences in the length of adolescence and in the age of onset and completion. While the physical changes of pubescence signal the beginning of this phase, sociological criteria such as achievement of adult status and privileges, marriage, the end of education and the beginning of economic independence frequently mark the termination of adolescence. The stage of adolescence is likely to end earlier in primitive cultures and later in technological ones.

In the present study an adolescent was defined as any individual, who was in the age group 13 to 19 years. The term adolescence was used to refer to the period between 13 years and 19 years of age, irrespective of all other criteria determining the onset and termination of this phase.

Socialization of a Girl in India

With reference to India, individuals who qualify to be called adolescents according to the above definition, do not necessarily exhibit the psychosocial and behavioural characteristics of adolescents as depicted in literature and mass media. Adolescence as a distinct developmental phase is not recognized in rural India. It is primarily an urban phenomenon, being partly a by-product of Westernization in India and partly of the education system which, in a sense, postpones the onset of adult responsibilities.

In the traditional Indian set up, the period after childhood is devoted to learning of adult skills and responsibilities, more so among girls. This is particularly true of the lower income groups which constitute 40 per cent of the population. Whether or not the girl goes to school, she has very few choices, sometimes none, with regard to her life pattern. Limited resources and clear adult expectations enable her to go through her adolescence without much conflict about life goals. In general, the number of choices in life increase with the level of socioeconomic status (SES). Thus middle and upper SES adolescents are likely to confront situations that involve making decisions which can create increasingly more conflicts.

The identity of an Indian teenage girl differs in many ways from that of her Western counterpart, whose profile is familiar to students of developmental psychology from text books and other material. The Indian girl experiences puberty and the related physical and physiological changes without necessarily being burdened with the issue of identity achievement. This is partly because her identity is wholly defined by her relationship to others, specially to the members of her family. Irrespective of her individual needs and potential she is expected to inculcate culturally designated 'virtues' of womanhood. Submission and docility in conduct as well as skill and grace in performing household tasks are cherished values. Individualism as known in the West is not valued or tolerated. Conformity to the family's value system in order to maintain group identity is considered important.

The training of the girl is aimed at turning her into a good daughter-in-law, obedient, skilful, and demure. As soon as she is past her childhood (approximately 6 years old) the mother begins to involve her in household responsibilities including cooking, cleaning and care of younger siblings. There is a direct shift from the playfulness of childhood to responsibilities of adulthood. The irony in an Indian girl's life is that to be a good daugther-in-law and a worthy wife she must be more than ever the perfect daughter. Her chances of a fine marriage are damaged if she displays inclinations contrary to those traditionally desired. The danger of such a possibility indirectly monitors the girl's behaviour towards that which is socially approved, because she is brought up to view marriage as the major goal in life.

According to the Census of India 1981, 43.47 per cent girls in the age group 15-19 years were married. Girls who receive formal education beyond the primary level tend to be married later. The fact that these girls do not drop out of school after the Vth standards suggests a positive value placed on education by the family. Families that recognise the need for the education of the girls would not generally emphasise early marriage for them. Hence the marriage of educated girls normally takes place in their late teens or early twenties. In urban areas the period of formal education is longer and the age at marriage is higher than in rural areas. Once married, girls are rarely permitted to continue their education, except in a few middle or upper class urban families.

Considering that the girl is married in early adolescence and sent to her husband's house soon after puberty, she is still an adolescent as a bride. While she is adjusting to the unfamiliar set up at her new home, she is also coping with the post pubescent bodily changes that produce feelings and sensations that are unfamiliar. At a time when she would like to share confidences and seek advice from those who care, she is surrounded by people with whom she must maintain a respectful distance. The process of feminine development is incomplete at the time an Indian girl gets married (Kakar, 1978).

In an urbanised and industrialised set up, there are many opportunities for boys and girls of marriageable age to come into contact with each other, as in college and neighbourhoods. But these interactions and acquaintances are not expected to become romantic or lead to marriage. If a romantic involvement occurs, parents on both sides try to persuade their children to drop their choices unless the partners have suitable *jati*, *gotra*, and social status. If a girl defies her parents, they sever their relations with her; but this is usually a rare occurrence.

Traditionally, in a marriage arranged by the parents, the girl herself has little or no role to play in the selection of her mate. She is rarely informed when the search for the groom begins. She may get a clue about it, but is too embarrassed to ask anything. Her consent is not sought when the groom is finally selected; it is assumed that she will agree. Even if the mother asks her, it is a mere formality, as the girl is not expected to say 'no'. She simply agrees. If the girl has any reservations, she has no voice, for questioning elders about one's own marriage is considered immodest.

In educated and urbanised middle and upper class families, where girls have also pursued higher education, girls play a more active role in the selection of their partners. Their opinions carry weight and they are usually not forced to marry anyone against their wishes. However, even in these cases, the need for parental approval is very strong. If the girl finds a partner herself she is allowed to marry provided the parents approve of the alliance and go through the ritual of arranging it themselves. It has generally been found that girls prefer their marriage to be arranged by their parents. They only want the right of veto : the prerogative to decline an offer if the person does not appeal to them (Cormack, 1961(a); Mathew, 1960; Sheth, 1972).

The whole issue of marriage-when to marry and whom to marry is believed to be of critical importance in the identity formation of an adolescent in Erikson's theory. According to him the young person must visualise and seek the kind of person he or she wants to marry (1968). When the final decision for marriage rests upon the young persons themselves, dating and courtship, which are Western norms of behaviour, precede marriage. They may choose to marry or reject the person they date; hence the choice is theirs. Conflicts in the face of many choices are expected, resulting in a state of confusion.

Since most Indian girls have no choice in this domain, marriage may not produce an identity crisis in the same way as it does for Western adolescents. However marriage does signify an abrubt change without a transition from one stage (childhood) to another (adulthood), so that the girl has to revise her self image, fit herself into the role defined for her and create a place for herself in a family whose members may pick on her at the slightest opportunity. She would have come with the intention to please her husband and his parents. However, she cannot avoid feeling alienated. The constant strain of maintaining appropriate behaviour makes her resentful towards her parents-in-law in the beginning who first test her abilities and endurance before accepting her.

The crisis lasts until the girl is able to establish herself as an obedient and dutiful daughter-in-law, whose presence in the house would not threaten family solidarity. In Kakar's words, "the identity struggle of the adolescent Indian girl is confounded by the coincidence of marriage, the abrupt and total severance of the attachments of childhood and her removal from all that is familiar to a state of lonely dependency upon a household of strangers" (1978, P.76). Of course, this is true of societies which have village exogamy.

The need to be economically independent is considered to be one of the factors contributing to the crisis of identity at adolescence. While the value of education for girls has increased gradually over the years, the emphases on norms and goals prescribed for them have not changed. Despite high school or university education, girls are not expected to be vocationally oriented or ambitious of a career. A girl's education is seen to have two main values. It adds to her matrimonial qualification, and to her ability to supplement income or shoulder financial responsibility.

In towns and cities economic pressures as well as urbanisation have increased the need for employment of women. Since most jobs have a certain level of education and training as a prerequisite, girls in increasing numbers are going in for higher education.

One unavoidable consequence of higher education among girls is the need to work outside the home. The ambition of educated girls to be able to earn is all pervasive. They want to contribute to the family resources, prove their worth and sometimes exercise power over decisions in the family. However, total economic independence of girls is not encouraged in most families. Very few are allowed to take up white collar jobs, especially in rural areas, where going to work may mean going outside the home and farm to the nearest town a couple of miles away.

When a girl who has received formal education upto high school is denied any opportunity for self enhancement, she probably has ideological conflicts. On the one hand, education and school experience give her a taste of independence; on the other hand, family restrictions curb any move made to become individualistic. Once educated, the girl is aware of the hypothetical choices open to her, although she may not be able to turn to any of them. Thus, being educated and then vocationally qualified is likely to produce many conflicts which would affect the girl's identity.

It is necessary to explain the presence of a fairly large number of women force in employment, specially in urban areas. Whether educated or not, most women who work do so due to economic pressures on the family. If their families were not pressed for increasing their economic resources, they probably would not be allowed to work. Only a small minority among the upper middle class are working for personal satisfaction. Once married, the decision regarding her employment rests with the woman's husband and his family. Thus employment outside the home is largely not a part of the girl's social identity in India. In other words, career choices would not contribute towards identity confusion at adolescence for girls in the same way as they would for boys.

Significant to the identity of an Indian are some cultural themes that seem to characterise the whole of Indian society (Kakar, 1978; Mandelbaum, 1972; NIPCCD, 1980). These are amalgamated in the experience of any child growing up here. The socialisation practices prevalent across regions reflect as well as reinforce the tendency to adhere to these themes. With minor subcultural variations, the themes that pertain to the majority can be approximately summarised as follows.

Network of Hierarchies

Male Supremacy

As is the unwritten law in many cultures the male in India is regarded as unquestionably superior to the female. He is vested with greater authority over family decisions and resources than the woman. Both women and children are expected to be respectful towards and in awe of the menfolk. Men may even rebuke their wives without apparent feelings of guilt or regret. The sense of inferiority of the female is quite pervasive.

The woman's status improves with the birth of a son but deteriorates if she produces a daughter. Since the son is her social redeemer she indulges him and invests herself in his future, creating a deep emotional bond with him.

Age hierarchy

In the Indian tradition a person can wield control over people younger to him by virtue of his age alone. Thus not only do fathers have formal authority over their sons and daughters, but older brothers also command deference from their younger ones. Respect for age and experience is undisputed across the regions in India.

However, where women are concerned, this principle does not hold true in the same way. Not all older women can expect deference from the younger males and females, the variance being produced by the nature of kin relationships. For example, a mother-in-law reigns supreme over her daughter-in-law by virtue of age and status but a man's sister, even if younger than his wife, actually has more authority over his wife.

The theme of male superiority cuts across the theme of age hierarchy in the female world. It is not uncommon for a younger brother to keep vigilance over his older sister's activities, specially if she is an adolescent and unmarried. He has parental support in this exercise as any 'untoward' act on the girl's part is likely to tarnish her reputation and bring a "bad name" to the family.

At a later age, a woman's authority usually depends on her husband's position in the household. In general it is understood that "the eldest male of the higher generation is supposed to receive the most respect and obedience, the female at the opposite pole, the most protection and care" (Orenstein, quoted in Mandelbaum, 1972, P.40).

Caste hierarchy

The third major hierarchical system that plays a significant role in determining the identity of a Hindu in India is his caste. The fourfold system of 'Varna' as laid down by Manu in Hindu scriptures is not that specific, it is the *jati* system that is the frame of reference. Every village is inhabited by members of several *jatis*. A member of a *jati* would normally participate in the traditional occupation, marry within his group and follow the *jati* norms for relating with other groups.

Family loyality

In the traditional Indian family there is great emphasis on loyalty to the family. The term family is often used to refer to the group that includes all the members of the patrilineal kin. Each member must remember, while conducting himself in the outside world, that he is a representative of his family and not simply an individual. He should refrain from socially disapproved behaviour or activities not only to protect his own reputation but also to maintain the honour of his family. Individual needs and expressions are considered secondary to the family needs and any action that threatens the family unity is dealt with immediately. Conformity to family ideals is generally admired.

Any person who is not related is regarded as more distant and friendships outside kinship are given legitimacy by the use of kinship terms. Thus a male friend may be referred to as a brother and a neighbour as an uncle and so on.

In times of economic or emotional crises in the lives of any members, the remaining members are expected to serve as shock absorbers, pool their own resources and see their kinsmen through hard times with equal responsibility. If help is sought outside the family when it is available at home, it is considered a direct insult to family integrity.

Belief in fate/destiny

A traditional Indian belief about the human experience is that what is to happen is preordained, man only being a medium to achieve this goal. A child is believed to be born with a destiny or fate of his own. His achievements or lack of these are attributed to his innate disposition rather than to his own strivings.

In the face of these beliefs a child's socialisation is leavened with faith in his own potentialities and inherent limits. He is allowed to mature at his own pace, without any undue emphasis on developmental milestones and learning of tasks. In a subtle way, there is greater recognition of individual differences among children in this attitude than what the Western concept of control of environmental variables permits.

Considerations in Socialisation

In an Indian family, no other period of life is as carefree as that of infancy and early childhood. The child is considered the 'gift of God' and nurtured with indulgence. The mother is the primary source of his physical ministrations and emotional gratification. The Indian mother tends to follow rather than lead her child in dealing with his inclinations and with the tempo of development (Kakar, 1978). Culturally it is believed that the child will mature at his own pace; hence there is no deliberate effort to make him autonomous.

However, around the age of 5 or 6, the child experiences an abrupt weaning from the world of maternal protection to a series of responsibilities. Expectations from boys and girls begin to diverge, both being socialised for their respective sex roles.

While the girl still remains under the surveillance of the mother, the boy is initiated into the man's world where standards of conformity are uncompromising and relentless. The girl is given specific household chores and responsibilities so that by the time she is 11 or 12 years old she has become proficient in the affairs of the house. Although the boy is still relatively free from such pressing role taking, his liberty is considerably curtailed and parental affection is made contingent upon his good behaviour.

The technique of disciplining the child is guided by the belief that a child should not be praised to his face as this will make him conceited. Apart from this, praising one's own child may be seen as a display of parental vanity, a trait that goes against cultural norms. In general, punishment or threats of physical punishment for transgression are used to control children's behaviour. The child learns to differentiate between right and wrong, or acceptable and unacceptable behaviour from his experiences of negative reinforcement rather than from reward. Other people's opinions, fear of social stigma and threat to family prestige are held out as the monitors of the code of conduct.

In sum, the Indian tradition may be said to include features such as acceptance of male superiority, respect for age, hierarchy of castes, value for loyalty to the family, belief in destiny and an indulgent attitude towards very young children. These themes have historicity as well as current validity and, therefore, constitute a significant part of the traditional culture.

Defining Traditionality and Modernity

The term 'traditional' used in this study needs to be operationally defined, as there is some ambiguity as to the meaning of this term. In common usage it has been contrasted to the term 'modern'. It may be of conceptual relevance to point out that in this discussion, the traditional person or society is not perceived as the antithesis of the modern. In fact, the two entities are visualised as complementary rather than mutually exclusive.

The term tradition refers to all that we inherit from the past. Shils (1971) defines tradition as beliefs with a particular consensus through time. It is a collective memory transmitted through the ages, although, everything of the past does not become tradition. As a matter of fact, only a few elements of our social heritage are regarded as tradition. In other words, a process of selection is implied in the passing down of tradition. People in any given period do not incorporate all that their past generations did or said. If this were to happen social inheritance would become bulky and cumbersome. Only some actions are selected, and the selection presupposes a value system.

It is apparent that a traditional person is one who follows the traditions of his society. Like culture and language, tradition is also related to a particular group of people. It is a force that binds a set of people together. In a sense every man is traditional to the extent that he is the product of an interaction between his inherent tendencies, his own history and his society's history. Conveying a similar view, Erikson had (1958) remarked :

> We cannot even begin to encompass a human being without indicating for each of the stages of his life cycle the framework of social influences and of traditional institutions which determine his perspectives on his more infantile past and on his more adult future (P.18).

Modernity can be viewed as a construct that connotes revision of existing traditions and anticipation of new and better practices. It is not erasing of everything old; conversely every change is not a step towards modernity. "Only a change which affects our traditions in the sense of a richer modification, can be regarded as a sign of modernity" (Ganguly, 1977, P.52). A modern man, then, is not a man without traditions, but a man with traditions adapted to contemporary living. When man utilises his creative imagination to modify his traditions, he is truly working towards modernity.

Quite often tradition has been viewed as an impediment to technological advancement and hence to modernity. Sometimes society has to face rapidly changing situations, material or non material. Technical achievements often present situations to which a people have to readjust quickly, that is, modify their traditions in an unusually short period. In this process modernity appears to be a synonym of technological advancement. Considering the pace at which traditions have to change, it may appear that traditions tend to clash with modernity. It is however, not tradition *per se* but the institutionalisation of tradition that comes into conflict with modernity. An exercise to change traditional values without a corresponding change in the structural aspects (occupational and educational systems) is likely to meet with failure (Anandalakshmy, 1973).

A person who is tradition bound has hardly any reservations against technical advancement. The experience of modern Indian industry has shown that traditional labour can adapt itself to the needs of machine technology without much effort and that the occupational orientation of castes has not been a major handicap. One significant psychological reason could be the sense of security the traditional man enjoys. He may be "submerged in collectivity, but he is clear about his identity and has a sense of belonging" (Anandalakshmy, 1973, P.2). Those who have alienated themselves from tradition, e.g. the *nouveau riche*, in blind pursuit of a material culture, and also have tried to keep their identity by holding on to certain older institutions are the ones who hinder the growth of modernity in the culture.

Tradition imparts a cultural identity to a person. It guides him in his social life and in understanding his fellow beings. Hence an individual who is traditional is likely to experience a greater sense of identity than a person who, by dint of rejection of his traditions, aspires to be 'modern'. Traditionality, by definition, encompasses a set of value orientations that enable the individual to identity himself as one who subscribes to them. A sense of uprootedness which, according to Erikson (1968), is a sure sign of loss of identity, tends to pervade in cases where there is a negation or obliviousness of the past and the future is not quite known.

Continuing the same argument it may be said that a traditional person is not necessarily less modern or vice versa. It is possible for a person to be traditional in one sphere and modern in another. The two constructs denote social psychological orientations that may exists in parallel.

Several socio-psychological characteristics have been delineated by sociologists that, according to them, cluster together to make up a traditional man. However, there seems to be no rationale of the basis on which he is referred to as traditional, since the emphasis in these studies has been on isolating the syndrome of modernity or looking for the 'modern man'. The traits antithetical to the 'modern man' were labelled as 'traditional'. Two important variables, rural urban residence and socio-economic status are studied in this context and have relevance to the present study.

Rural-Urban Residence

Several studies of modernisation investigating levels of modernity have found urban living and urban experience to be significantly correlated with modernity (Inkeles and Smith, 1974; Lerner, 1958; Portes, 1973; Schnaiberg, 1970(a), (b)). According to this body of research urban residence is instrumental in increasing the availability of the institutional network that exerts a modernising influence.

Frequently the urban man is described as modern and the rural as traditional. However, the same studies also define modernity in a way that the definition is already biased in favour of urban living because of the other elements associated with it. Findings questioning the validity of the relationship have also been reported. Inkeles and Smith (1974) in their large scale study on modernity expected, by their own measure, that those living in the more cosmopolitan cities would prove to be more modern. However, the authors did not find any statistically significant evidence of this nature consistently across even in one of the six countries studied. It was their conclusion that it is not the urban experience *per se* which makes men more modern, but rather their differential contact with other institutions and change agents such as schools, mass media, and factories which the cities contain.

Socio-economic Status

Socio-economic status (SES) as a variable has also been examined in relation to modernity. Kahl (1968) expressed the view that social status was a better predictor of 'modernism'* than was provincial versus urban residence. In his study of modernism across Brazil and Mexico (1968) Kahl found that once position in the social structure was controlled, there were no significant differences between different nations on the level of modernism.

A high correlation between SES indicators and the modernity index was also reported by Portes (1973) supporting Kahl's earlier assertion that socioeconomic status was the primary determinant of the emergence of modern attitudes. Occupation and income, which are two important status indicators, also signify the potential freedom and exposure to new experiences available to the individual by virtue of his work situation. The third factor, education, plays a dual role as a status indicator and as a direct measure of the amount of knowledge (Portes, 1973). In the absence of information on income, the place of dwelling (type of neighbourhood) can act as a status indicator.

A link between higher SES (hence affluence) and modernity of attitudes seems to make sense. Implied in the same conceptual framework is the hypothesis that those on the lower rungs of the SES ladder are less modern; in other words, more traditional. In the studies of modernity, the traditional man (who is also most often the poor man) is known to be fatalistic rather than one with a sense of personal efficacy. However, his fatalism is not a cause of his traditional attitudes and hence of poverty. Believing so would be tantamount to treating a consequent as an antecedent (Anandalakshmy, 1973). A low economic level means a low control over economic resources, leading to negligible access to services and privileges in society. In these circumstances it is pragmatic for a poor man to believe that forces outside of him have more control over his resources than he does himself. He classifies this powerlessness under a culturally acceptable label, 'Fate'.

It is not a matter of chance that the components that characterise an economically poor society (high death rate, low life expectancy, a

* Kahl uses this term to denote modernity.

higher proportion of people in the younger age groups, a low level of education and literacy, unemployment and underemployment, low wages, absence of saving etc.) are found to overlap with the traits of a traditional society, e.g. the Indian society. The etiology of this myth (traditional, therefore, poor) could be traced to the way the tools measuring traditionality-modernity have defined and measured these dimensions. The tradition-modernity continuum (a controversial concept) often coincides with the poverty-affluence continuum (which is unilinear). Thus in this model, poverty gets equated with traditionality and affluence with modernity. For the same reason there is a need to separate the concept of tradition from poverty and conservatism, and to remove the negative loading associated with being truly traditional.

The Present Study

In the present study, keeping in view the cultural themes and the issues of importance to an Indian, a person (an adolescent girl in this case) was regarded traditional if she :

a) Attributed most events in life to fate rather than to personal effort;

b) Believed in caste allegiance and caste distinctions;

c) Credited the male and the female with culturally prescribed sex roles;

d) Endorsed preference for male children over female children;

e) Was committed totally to family solidarity and values;

f) Endorsed age hierarchy in relationships; and

g) Supported the traditional practice in the arrangement and performance of the marriage ritual.

The objective of the present study was to investigate whether demographic, social and psychological correlates such as rural-urban residence, socio-economic status and traditionality exert any influence on the identity of adolescent girls.

It was hypothesized that adolescent girls who are traditional in their orientation, irrespective of their place of dwelling and socio economic status, are more fully identified with their sex roles and socially assigned statuses than those who are less traditional. It was further predicted that factors interfering in the girl's identity crystallisation at adolescence are formal education and related vocational aspirations, choice in marriage and delayed marriage.

2

Description of Adolescent Subjects

A total of 150 girls in the age group 16 to 19 years were interviewed in depth for the study. There were 60 subjects from rural areas and 90 from urban areas, selected from lower, middle and upper socio-economic status groups. Age and sex were the only two criteria determining the universe from which the subjects were selected. The Purposive Sampling method was used to identify girls. The independent variables that determined the inclusion of girls in the sample were (a) rural/urban residence and (b) socio-economic status. Marital status was not a criterion for selection, and the sample, therefore, had both married and unmarried adolescent girls.

For determining the SES level of subjects, no previously standardised socio-economic status scale was found satisfactory (Aaron, *et al.*, 1969; Pareek and Trivedi, 1964; Shirpurkar, 1967). In the scales reviewed it was found that different status indicators were treated as equivalent to each other and given equal numerical scores. Thus possessing a chair was equal to have a radio or a bullock cart. The Kuppuswamy Scale of SES (1962) for urban populations was also not found suitable. The revised version had been developed almost five years earlier and was not found to reflect the existing standard of living.

In view of these limitations, certain criteria were developed to determine the three SES categories used in the study. In the rural areas these were, occupation of the head of the family and size of land holding. For urban families the criteria were occupation of the head of the family and locality of residence.

Support for the method comes from a research bibliography (Glenn *et al.*, 1970) in which occupation has been shown to be the best single predictor of social status. Type of house and dwelling area were also stated to be highly correlated with social status.

The distribution of subjects in terms of socio-economic status and rural urban residence is seen in Table-1.

Table-1
Distribution of Rural and Urban Subjects in three Socio-economic Statuses.

	Rural		Urban	Total
SES	Punjab	Uttar Pradesh	Delhi	
Lower	15	15	30	60
Middle	15	15	30	60
Upper	-	-	30	30
Total	30	30	90	150

The Rural Sample

Rural subjects were selected from the states of Punjab and Uttar Pradesh. Thirty adolescent girls, 15 from lower SES and 15 from middle SES, were studied in each state. These two northern states of India are known to differ from each other both in subculture and economy, Punjab being more affluent. It was, therefore, estimated that a study of rural girls in these two subcultures would be valuable in assessing the roles of two slightly varying settings in the identity formation of girls.

In Punjab the study was conducted in district Gurdaspur, the subjects being drawn from 13 villages in the area. The reason for such a spread out sampling is that most of the middle SES subjects (13) were selected from a school they were attending in one of the villages. The school was attended by students from many villages around it. In Uttar Pradesh most of the subjects (23) were from village Ismail Ganj, which is situated 8 kilometres north-east of Lucknow. The remaining seven subjects were construction labourers on a building site in Lucknow, being rural migrants from villages in Uttar Pradesh.

In Table-2 are presented some of the demographic characteristics of the rural girls so that an idea about them can be derived.

Table-2
Some Demographic Characteristics of the Rural Sample

SES N=15 in each group	Level of education	Average number of children in family		No. married.
		M	F	
Lower SES - Punjab	Std. IV to X	2.3	3.5	NIL
Lower SES - U.P	Nil to Std.VIII	2.0	3.3	10
Middle SES - Punjab	High School	1.3	3.5	NIL
Middle SES - U.P	Middle to High School	2.4	3.3	4

The category of rural upper SES was not included in the study for two reasons. One, it was expected that in any one village there would be very few families that one could term "upper class", since that would be defined only by their caste and affluence. However, given the definition of SES in this study these affluent upper-caste families would not necessarily qualify. For instance, whether a cultivator owned 10 acres or 50 acres of land, his social status would still be that of a cultivator. Selecting upper SES subjects in rural areas would have thus posed sampling problems. Secondly, it is known that in the rural enviornment the middle and upper socio-economic groups are fairly congruent in their values, ways of life and socialisation practices.

The Urban Sample

In Delhi 90 adolescent girls were the subjects for this study, 30 girls from each of lower, middle and upper SES levels. Six of the girls in the lower SES were married, all others being unmarried.

3

Tools for Data Collection

It was hypothesized in the study that the level of traditionality of a girl would influence her identity. Hence a measure was needed to ascertain this.

Keeping in view the cultural settings and the varied educational levels of the proposed subjects, a questionnaire was developed to assess the standing of the adolescent subjects on a scale measuring traditionality. It was prepared carefully in consultation with several social scientists and experts, who were requested to assess each item for its cultural and objective relevance. Ideas for construction were taken from several other existing scales without using any of their items in toto*.

The Questionnaire (Appendix I)

The questionnaire was entitled Attitudes on Issues of Social Significance, an appropriate title and one that would comouflage its purpose. It was felt that if the title of the questionnaire clearly indicates that it purports to measure the extent of traditionality, social desirability would influence the responses.

There were 35 items in the questionnaire. The items were based on seven issues, namely, discrimination between sexes, male-female status in marriage, marriage customs, family loyalty vs individualism, caste attitudes, age hierarchy, and fatalism vs personal efficacy. These areas were construed to be culturally relevant and related to the major issues under study.

* Armer, (1970), Kahl (1968), Schnaiberg (1979 (b).

Under each of the seven issues five items were constructed, thus making a total of 35 items. Further, every item contained two polar statements, one reflecting the "traditional" stereotype [part (a)] and the other expressing the "non-traditional" viewpoint [part (b)]. The questionnaire had three columns. Column I and Column III listed part (a) and part (b) statements respectively. The middle column contained three boxes, namely A, In-between, and B. If the subject agreed with statement (a) she was expected to place a tick mark in box A. If she agreed with statement (B) she was to place the mark in box B. If she did not completely agree with either of the two statements and felt that she preferred a middle ground between the two, she could fill the "in-between" box.

The scale was prepared both in English and Hindi. For those who could not read either language, the statements were read out and the responses were filled in by the researchers. When conducting the study in Punjab, the statements were translated into Punjabi by the researcher.

The "traditional" and "non-traditional" statements were not always placed in columns I and II respectively. The order was jumbled up so that sometimes it was the 'non-traditional belief' in column I and sometimes it was the "non traditional belief". Care was taken not to place them in any pattern. Another technique introduced to disguise the scale was to not to group together items from the same category. Item No.1 from each area was taken and these seven items were placed one after the other. This order was repeated till all the five items from each of the seven categories were listed. It was hoped that such techniques of questionnaire construction would minimize the possibility of the social desirability effect, generally encountered in the questionnaire method.

The Interview Schedule (Appendix II)

The most important part of the study was to obtain sufficient information from the subjects that would reveal how well-identified they were with their status and sex-role. Known measures of identity used in the United States (Constantinople, 1975; Marcia, 1975) were not found to be adequate or appropriate to collect in-depth data.

An interview schedule consisting of 48 open ended questions was developed. This schedule was in four parts. The first part of eight questions dealt with educational and vocational history and interests as well as future aspirations of the young women being interviewed. There were separate sets of questions for those studying in school/college and those who had either discontinued early or never entered school. This section was selected to form the first part of the interview as the theme was fairly non-controversial and hence, conducive to establishing rapport with the girls.

The second section included 18 questions on the socialisation of the girl. The focus of the interview was on identifying the domains in which sex discrimination between siblings was observed, the way in which this was expressed and the subjects' attitudes towards it. Apart from this there were questions related to the girl's status in her family. The degree of independence given to her, parental expectations, and her satisfaction/dissatisfaction with her sex-role and life circumstances. It was expected that responses to these questions would indicate the state of a girl's identity as it had emerged upto that point.

The third set of questions were on menarche and experiences related to it. Through nine questions subjects were asked about the onset of menarche, taboos related to menstruation, physical, mental and emotional changes as well as parental restrictions accompanying sexual maturation. The objecitve was to elicit the subjects' perception of female sexuality, particularly their own, and to determine the role of pubertal changes in identity formation.

The last part of the interview schedule dealt with the issue of marriage. There were 13 questions, their content being framed differently for the unmarried, married and those betrothed to be married. Discussions in this area were anticipated to prove the adolescent girl's actual and desired role in decisions regarding her marriage, her perception of roles and responsibilities after marriage, and her feelings or anticipated acceptance of them.

Piloting the Tools

Initial versions of the questionnaire and the interview-schedule were tested on five lower SES subjects. Following this, minor changes were introduced in the interview schedule while the contents of the questionnaire were changed considerably, introducing the present system of scoring. Both the tools were then used to study a lower class and an upper class adolescent girl.

The questionnaire was administered to 46 undergraduate students in a women's college. The girls belonged to upper-middle to upper SES, had good academic record and were studying subjects that would predispose them to "non-traditional" views. Considering these features it was hypothesized that they would emerge fairly 'non-traditional' on the scale of traditionality. Their scores ranged from 1 to 15 with a mean score of 6.91. This dispersion indicated a non-traditional disposition of the students, and confirmed the face-validity of the scale.

That the questionnaire had predictive value was confirmed by the trends in results (see P.82). As an academic exercise and to provide a further check on its predictability, the questionnaire was again administered, two years later, to a fresh set of 41 undergraduate and postgraduate students attending the same courses. The range of scores was found to be 2 or 18 with a mean score of 7.63. These scores indicated a similarity between the traditionality levels of two different samples that were only temporally different, being similar on most other variables.

Procedure for Data Collection

After a subject had been contacted the researcher spent some time with her, and in many cases with the family also, explaining the purpose of the interview and nature of the research. While educated subjects did not take long to comprehend the purpose, those with lower levels of education or none at all required more explanation. They also needed greater persuasion before giving their consent for the interviews.

Quite often the interviews did not take place on the first day. The interview had to be conducted only when the subject was free for at least two hours and when she considered it convenient to her. As a result of this time lag some girls, previously contacted, refused to be available at the promised time due to one reason or the other. The dropout rate was higher among rural and lower SES groups than among the others. In most such cases other members of family rather than the girl herself appeared to be responsible, as they objected to her being interviewed by an outsider.

Of the 150 subjects, 120 were interviewed either in their own homes or in their neighbours' or friends' houses. In Punjab, 13 subjects were interviewed in their school premises while another 11 were interviewed in the farms where they worked as labourers. In Delhi, six girls from a women's college were interviewed in the college premises.

It was observed that in lower and middle SES families, the girl alone did not decide whether she would be willing to be a subject for the study. Her parents, older siblings, younger brothers, uncles and aunts and grandparents exercised considerable control over her decisions. When ever they declined consent for interview, the girl refused to be a subject. Although the reason was not elucidated, it could be surmised on the basis of reports by other girls that their relatives did not like their adolescent daughters or daughters-in-law talking alone to a stranger, fearing it might be some sort of family-planning propaganda. Sometimes an outspoken daughter was prevented from being interviewed lest she might give away too much about her family.

The Interview

When the subject appeared comfortable with responding to the questions, preliminary base-line data about her and her family were noted. If the subjects could read and follow either Hindi or English, the questionnaire was given to her to complete in the researcher's presence. It was never given away to be filled in at any other time or left overnight with the subject. If she could not read, the researcher read out the statements and filled in the responses, explaining the querry, only if clarification was demanded. The only exception was made in the case of lower SES subjects. Their questionnaires were filled in by the researcher irrespective of whether they could read or not in order to maintain uninformity in the procedure within that group.

While the interview was conducted, it was recorded on a cassette tape with a portable tape recorder. The girls were assured of absolute confidentiality with regard to the recorded material. On the whole, it was found that subjects, even those from whom the researcher anticipated apprehensions of this method, were not averse to the conversation being taped. A few subjects liked the recorder to be shut off for certain portions of the interview. The information was subsequently noted down after the interview. Most of the girls became unselfconscious about the tape recorder within minutes of starting the interview. For one thing, the recorder had a built-in microphone thus avoiding the need of the subject having to speak into a microphone. Almost all of them were aware of the functions of a tape recorder, though some of them had not seen it working.

In general, the order in which the questionnaire and the interview were completed was not fixed. Depending upon the flow of prior conversation and presence or absence of other members of family in the room, discretion was used to employ one technique or the other first. Care was taken not to hold the interview in the presence of any other person in the room or within hearing distance, if held in an open space. Sometimes the interview was discreetly discontinued and completed on another day. However, the attempt normally was to complete the whole procedure for one subject in one sitting. There was danger of the subject changing her mind about being interviewed or not getting time later or of being prevented by the mother (or others) to be interviewed a "second time".

The tone of the interview was as informal as possible, and resembled a conversation. Sometimes the order of questions would be altered in keeping with the direction of the conversation. The subjects were allowed to elaborate their statements and to express themselves freely. They could relate anecdotes and accounts of personal experiences. The interviews in Punjab were conducted in Punjabi while those in Uttar Pradesh and with lower and middle SES subjects in Delhi were conducted in Hindi. Most of the interviews with upper class subjects were in English.

On an average, the time taken to complete the questionnaire ranged from 15 to 30 minutes. The interview time varied from half-an-hour to two hours, being determined by the subjects' inclination to talk, and to give the details she wanted to include. Thus, after a girl had been prepared to be a subject it took anything from one hour to two-and-a-half hours to complete the session. In general, the length of the session was directly related to socio-economic status, with the higher levels taking more time.

Analysis of Data

To assess the effect of SES and rural-urban residence on the level of traditionality a one-way analysis of variance was computed.

The data from the interviews were descriptive and were therefore not coded. The responses under each subheading were noted down and analysed for their meaning and implications. Within each group a profile of a girl was drawn for effective illustration of the identity of the girl in that group. Comparisons were made across groups to determine intergroup differences. A detailed analysis of data was carried out to examine the general life patterns of rural and urban girls, their satisfaction with their own life styles and the implications of their attitudes in mental health terms.

4

Socialisation : The Experience of Being Female

It was while probing the domain of socialization that the adolescent girls communicated their awareness and resentment of being second to male children. A majority of girls reported that there were differences in the way daughters and sons were brought up in their own homes and in most other families. Table 3 gives the number of girls in each group who reported sex-discrimination and the ways in which it was practiced frequently.

Most of the girls reported that there were more restrictions placed on them as compared to boys. While hardly any checks were placed on boys, girls were not allowed freedom of movement. Boys could go anywhere and return late without causing much annoyance to their parents. Restrictions on girls varied depending upon social class and rural-urban residence.

The *rural lower SES girls* could not mix with peers of their own sex. Affiliation with friends was not considered a positive trait for a girl. Thus 22 girls reported that their interactions with peers were very restricted. In fact many girls did not have a person whom they could call a friend. Many girls were not permitted to go out at all. Others could go alone only to a short distance within the village while some could go only if accompanied by another person. There were parental prescriptions also regarding the type of clothes they could wear.

Table-3

No. of Subjects Reporting Sex discrimination in Socialisation, N=150

Topic	*Rural*		*Urban*			
	Lower SES	*Middle SES*	*Lower SES*	*Middle SES*	*Upper SES*	*Total*
Differential treatment of boys and girls	24	22	17	17	14	94
How ? :						
a) greater strictness with girls	7	9	6	5	5	32
b) lack of freedom of girls	21	20	17	15	17	90
c) indulgence of boys	17	17	16	8	9	67

It was noted that even though the subjects reported socialization differences, they themselves did not appear to feel as discriminated against as it appeared to the observer. It was obvious that some of the girls not only tolerated indulgence towards boys, but also perpetuated it themselves, especially if the boys were their younger brothers. The rural subjects in the lower SES group had accepted the preference for male children as customary and they pointed out the usual reasons for this preference. The most common reason given was the parents' perception of their sons as potential bread-winners. The other reasons were said to be anticipation of separation from girls after their marriage and old age support from sons.

In the *rural middles SES*, restrictions on girls extended to control over their peer relations. Very few girls reported to having friends other than their cousins. Parents did not tolerate their daughters' friendhships with a peer who was not a relative. Visting a peer within the village was not always permitted. If at all they went to meet a friend on an errand, they had to return very soon.

A majority of the girls had to wear clothes that their parents chose. They could not wear something that was considered fashionable. Of the 13 girls who said that they made their own decisions about their clothing, 11 were school-going.

The middle SES rural girls were familiar with the tradition of preference for male offspring and attributed this to the same reasons given by their lower SES and urban counterparts. However, from the pattern of their responses it was apparent that many girls resented the preference shown towards their brothers, although half of them had accepted this discrimination as on integral part of their life.

The *urban lower SES subjects* too reported parental monitoring of their friendships with same-sex peers. Half of them said that they could not go out to the market etc. with friends. It was interesting that almost 50% of girls in this group resented the differential treatment given to them. The attitude of resentment or of acceptance of the discrimination was not apparently related to any other dependent variable such as level of education or male-female ratio at home or marital status.

The reasons attributed by the girls for preference towards sons were that parents viewed boys as economically productive and girls as financial liabilities, since their marriages involved a lot of expenditure. A few girls were skeptical as to whether sons would actually look after their parents in old age.

A majority of *urban middle SES girls* experienced more restrictions on themselves as compared to boys (Table 3) and a good number of them stressed that they would like freedom. Almost all the girls in this group were fairly articulate in enumerating the ways in which they were discriminated.

Table-4

Subjects' Acceptance/Resentment of Sex-differences in Socialisation, $N = 150$

Attitude	*Rural*		*Urban*			
	Lower SES	*Middle SES*	*Lower SES*	*Middle SES*	*Upper SES*	*Total*
Acceptance	27	15	12	19	14	87
Resentment	03	13	14	11	10	51
Neutral	-	02	04	-	06	12
Total	30	30	30	30	30	150

When asked why people generally wanted sons more than daughters, 11 girls attributed this to the boys' potential to support their parents in old age and 10 girls attributed it to their role as the carriers of family name from generation to generation. Anticipation of separation from girls and extra expenditure on them because of marriage rituals were also reported as the reasons for preference for male children.

Compared to lower SES girls, these girls had greater freedom outside the home. Many of them were allowed to go alone up to a short distance, say, to a friend's house or to the market. A few said they could take a bus within the city. Another six said that they could go out only if there was another person with them. No one said that she could not go out at all. The degree of interaction with peers was low in this group. There was a check maintained on many girls (13) as to whom their friends were. Visiting friends was permitted to quite a number of girls (17), but if they went out, they had to be back within a given time limit. Most of the girls themselves believed in keeping to a time limit. While visiting friends was not uncommon, going to see movies with them was rare.

Finally, in the *urban upper SES group*, discrimination between sons and daughters was reported by about half the sample (Table 3). Some girls were vehement that boys should also be expected to work in the house. The girls themselves often attended to errands outside the house and hence did not think it inappropriate to expect boys to work inside the house. The most commonly stated reason for less freedom of movement to girls was thought to be the vulnerability of girls to eve-teasing and physical harm, and not lack of parental faith in them.

They agreed that in general the birth of a male child was more welcome than the birth of a female. However, except in two cases (one was the second daughter and the other was the third daughter) all the girls felt that their own birth had been welcomed. They observed that their parents had never let them feel that they should have been sons, even if there were only daughters.

The reasons advanced for preference of male children by upper SES subjects were very similar to those given by others. A number of girls were skeptical whether their brothers would take good care of their parents, especially after their own marriage. For this reason and specially when the girl did not have a brother, she wished that she could remain unmarried and look after her parents in their old age. She obviously did not consider it possible to be married and to look after her parents.

Peers occupied an important place in the lives of these upper class adolescent girls. Since they were all school or college-going, they spent a major part of their day with their age-mates. Parents generally did not interfere in the selection of friends and permitted the girls to go out with their peers for shopping and movies, visiting shopping centres or going to the cinema with friends was quite common. However, they had to be back more or less by the stipulated time or before it was dark.

Many girls were allowed to go for mixed group parties, though they could not stay on very late. Only four girls mentioned that they had male friends and their parents did not mind this. While other girls wished to have acquaintance with boys, their parents did not permit this. Friction with parents over peer-group affiliations was not reported. The supremacy of allegiance to the family over peer-group loyalty among Indian adolescent girls has been reported by Islam (1976), Binepal (1980), Gulati (1980), and Kumar (1980).

Except for the upper SES urban girl, girls in other groups had low to medium contact with their peers. Low affiliation with persons not related through kin or caste is a very Indian feature and conforms to the cultural theme of family loyalty. Establishing emotional ties with and confiding in a person who is not a close relation is treated as a sign of disrespect of and a threat to family solidarity. Apart from this, the girl in a traditional family is not expected to be "idle" so that she can "sit and gossip" with other girls. She must keep working in the house. If housework is over she must sit down with embroidery or knitting rather than meet her peers for a chat.

In psychological terms, these prescriptions are ways and means of channelizing the energy of sexually maturing girls into socially approved behaviour in the absence of healthy heterosexual contact. Being occupied would "keep the girls from day-dreaming and fantasising about boys" - a notion that is generally not verbalized to the girls. They are kept busy with housework instead.

Parental injunctions to girls regarding how they must conduct themselves form an important part of a girl's socialisation. The subjects in this study had been asked as to what their parents generally emphasized with regard to their code of conduct. The responses are summarised in Table-5.

There was a clear indication in the results of the five groups that discrimination between boys and girls in socialisation was practised and had been noticed by the girls. Sex-differences in child rearing have also been reported by Bajaj (1973), George (1973), Gill (1974), Gulati (1981), Madan (1965), Mandelbaum (1972), Mathai (1972), Minturn & Lambert (1964), Murthy (1974), Sahai (1974), Vasudev (1974), and Yardi (1972). The studies on socialisation for competence found that in the craft groups studied, self-reliance and responsibility were stressed for girls and school attendance for boys. For boys, going to school was a major responsibility while girls had to manage the household and the younger siblings. The more tedious and less interesting tasks were allocated to girls. They had less chance for initiative than boys. On the whole girls were perceived as sojourners in their natal family.

Table-5

Parental Emphases on Code of Conduct for Girls as Perceived by Girls, *N*=150

	Rural			*Urban*		
Parental Injunctions	*Lower SES*	*Middle SES*	*Lower SES*	*Middle SES*	*Upper SES*	*Total*
Maintain 'good girl' image	2	13	6	5	5	31
Mind own business	9	8	8	5	-	30
Stay indoors	8	3	16	5	-	32
Show deference towards elders	-	8	4	5	8	25
Be sweet tempered/subdued	5	-	3	3	2	13
Be feminine	-	-	-	-	13	13
Dress simply	1	2	1	2	1	7
Strive to achieve	-	1	-	15	5	21

Note - Each girl gave more than one response.

Sensitivity to the discrimination emerged as a crucial antecedent of the girls' rejection of or low identification with their sex-role. Except the rural lower SES girls, the girls in all the other groups resented the preference shown to boys, specifically envying them for their freedom of physical movement. While the lower and middle SES girls accepted the differences in socialisation as the norm of the society and hence inevitable, the upper SES girls were less willing to concede a superior status to boys on principle. In general, it was the physical and social limitation of being a girl (not being able to do what a boy was allowed) that was resented, rather than femaleness itself. Housework, marriage and child bearing were commonly accepted as integral features of womanhood, the time of their occurrence being later in the higher socioe-conomic status.

It was mentioned above that the rural lower SES girls did not verbalise resentment of sex-discrimination, a finding also reported by Madan (1965). The girls had internalised societal norms, accepted the curbs on them and the bias in favour of male children as part of the larger system of rewards and incentives within the family. Their orientation was undoubtedly a product of their own socialisation and was conducive to identification with the sex-role and status assigned to them.

Parallel to that was identification of the urban upper SES girls with their roles. A majority were well-adjusted in their roles but not passively. They resisted the discriminatory practices, argued with their parents in favour of topics like inter-caste marriage and worked towards participation in family decisions. What facilitated a positive outcome of these interactions was a somewhat close rapport between the girls and their parents. The sex-differences in upbringing were more subtle than they were in other groups. Limitations on the girls' behaviour were all not very distinct. They were not faced with social and economic pressures to achieve. They felt that academic and vocational achievement was for personal progress and not so much to become more eligible for marriage, or to provide economic support to the family through a job. Their individual problems were not seen by them as basic to their being female.

Thus, it appeared that the upper SES girls preferred to be more emancipated as females rather than rejecting their own sex. They did not see it as an inherent property of womanhood to be subdued, secondary and unequal to the male. The fact that these girls could anticipate an occupational role, had some economic and volitional independence and the sanction to have a psychosocial moratorium meant that they could be individuals in their own right, though not being sufficiently individualistic would not cause anxiety. This enhanced in the girls a sense of self-esteem, an essential prerequisite for a positive sense of identity.

There was a basic difference in the nature of sex-role identification of the lower and upper SES girls. The girl in the lower group accepts the society's conception about herself, and hence does not feel any conflict between her needs and the requirements of her role. Instead she assumes that her needs will be fulfilled if she accepts a position generally oriented around the primacy of men. Her strong identification with the sex-role serves as a pillar of strength. This finds support in the study conducted by Lavoie (1976) who found that "high identity" (as measured through Marcia Ego Identity Status Scale) was positively related to sex-role identification.

Findings from the research study (Anandalakshmy, 1994) conducted on more than thirteen thousand girls across the country point to a dismal lack of change in the girl's situation in the last decade since the present study was completed. The findings revealed stark gender segregation within the family, with household tasks like sweeping and cooking being exclusively female tasks. The boys enjoyed more freedom in every sphere including in making friends with the opposite sex. The girls in the study felt that the value of their education would disappear once they were married.

5

Education and Aspirations : Engendering Dilemma

Formal education is believed to be a strong instrument of social change in a developing society. The government of India has made efforts to raise the level of education since independence. However, the literacy levels of females have continued to remain inferior compared to the males. Although the female enrolment rate at younger ages has improved, the dropout rate for girls remains high-compared to boys. According to the 1981 census there were 37.47 percent girls in the age group 10-14 years attending school compared to 62.07 percent boys. In the 14-17 age group only 15.61 percent girls as against 33.47 percent boys were attending school.

In the present study rural girls had a low level of formal education compared to urban girls. Further, the level of education improved with SES in both rural and urban samples. Tables 6 and 7 percent a profile of the patterns of formal education among rural and urban girls studied.

Table 6
Level of Formal Education of Lower and Middle SES Rural Girls, *N*=60

Level of Education	*Punjab*				*Uttar Pradesh*				*Total*
	Lower SES		*Middle SES*		*Lower SES*		*Middle SES*		
	Attending	Discontinue	Attending	Discontinue	Attending	Discontinue	Attending	Discontinue	
Std. V-VIII	-	10	-	2	1	3	-	7	23
High School	2	-	12	1	-	-	3	2	20
Intermediate	-	-	-	-	-	-	-	3	3
Total educated	2	10	12	3	1	3	3	12	46
Illiterate	3		-		11		-		14
Total Subjects	15		15		15		15		60

Table 7
Levels of Formal Education of Lower, Middle and Upper SES Urban Girls, *N*=90

Level of Education	*Lower SES*		*Middle SES*		*Upper SES*		*Total Educated*
	Attending	Discontinue	Attending	Completed Education	Attending	Discontinue	
1	2	3	4	5	6	7	8
Std. III-VIII	-	16	-	-	-	-	16
Std. IX - XII	8	4	21	01	12	-	46

(Contd.)

Table 7 (Contd.)

1	2	3	4	5	6	7	8
Bachelor's degree	-	-	07	01	18	-	26
Illiterate	02		-		-		02
Total subjects	30		30		30		90

The responses to the questions regarding educational aspirations and the benefits of education showed inter-group differences, across SES as well as between rural and urban groups. The illiterate subjects in rural areas mentioned that in their villages it was considered inappropriate for girls to attend school, although they themselves would have liked to get some education. Only two school-going girls aspired to the career of a teacher. The others either had no vocational aspirations, or simply wished to have more education. Generally, the girls did not consider school education as necessary for girls as it was for boys.

The value of being employed outside the home after some education was high in this group. Girls who were working as labourers felt that had they been educated, they might have been working under better conditions. Many girls considered literacy as instrumental in the ability to read and write letters etc.

The *middle SES rural Girls* were more educated and also more ambitious. For them education was high on priority. Apart from perceiving it as a symbol of higher status, they also saw it as a means to be relieved from the drudgery of housework and the nagging by parents and others at home. There were 14 girls who had discontinued education at different points. Financial difficulty in the family, lack of a school or college within reach, parents' unwillingness to permit further education and imminence of marriage were some of the reasons mentioned for dropping out of school. All the 14 girls indicated that they would have liked to continue their education had they been given a chance.

In this group a girl's formal education was regarded to have a significant role in determining the selection of her marriage partner.

Half the girls mentioned that the chances of finding a good match (educated and well-to-do) improved if the girl was educated upto 8th standard or more. A few girls (8) conveyed the impression that although education was good for girls, it posed a problem in their marriage, as the boy would have to be more educated than the girl and the demands for dowry increased with the boy's level of education.

Most of the middle SES rural girls (19) considered formal education equally necessary for girls and boys, although the remaining believed that education was less important for girls.

As Table 7 indicates, among the *urban lower SES families* 28 out of 30 girls were either attending school or had been to school and dropped out. The eight girls who were in school wanted to study beyond the higher_secondary level either to do a vocational course or to complete graduation. All of them wanted to take up jobs after their education, their aspirations varying from becoming a teacher,a typist or a telephone operator.

Formal education was considered equally necessary for both boys and girls by 17 out of 30 subjects in this sample. Educational qualification was perceived as a means of find a job by six school-going and eight non-school going girls. For many schooling meant picking up the basic ability to read and write letters, keep accounts and cope with situations. For some others education had wider implications. They said that it helped a person gain knowledge about the world, develop confidence and be able to guide their children in their studies. Seventeen girls stated that the level of education also influenced the selection of a suitable marriage partner positively.

In the *urban middle SES sample*, the girls placed high value on formal education. Education was considered equally essential for both boys and girls. Most of them said that the main objective of their education was to secure a job. Many girls wanted to join banks or government service. There were those who wanted to become teachers, lecturers or doctors. Everyone of them wanted to work outside the home and it was believed by them that their parents would not prevent them from taking up jobs.

Different reasons were given for wanting to work. Fourteen said that they wanted to be economically independent from their parents so that they did not have to depend on them to meet their own needs of expenditure. Working to help the family financially was also one of the reasons. Some wanted to work to make use of their education or 'enhance their personality' or just because it interested them.

The girl's education was seen as one of the important factors determinig her eligibility for marriage. While eight girls said that it was the primary factor looked into at the time of marriage, 14 girls mentioned that the educational level was only one of the several other important considerations.

The *upper SES urban girls* were the most highly educated among the 150 girls studied. While formal education was viewed as a menas to secure a job, many of them (15) also emphasised its intrinsic value in developing the personality. There were 26 girls who wanted to take up careers. A noticeable feature of the upper SES subjects was that all of them mentioned several options out of which they would finally select one. No one indicated very definitely that she wanted to pursue a particular profession, except one girl who was studying medicine. The final selection of any one line was subject to the girl's academic performance, her parents' approval and her success in the entrance examination, if any. The ambitions stated by the girls were quite closely related to their career aspirations.

While most of the upper SES girls thought that education was equally necessary for boys and girls, there were a few who considered it less important for girls to pursue higher education. These girls felt that it should be left to the girl to decide whether or not she wanted to study further after her schooling.

All the girls were receiving education, some formally in institutions and others informally in their homes and the community. However, the need for scholastic achievement, irrespective of its relevance in the socio-cultural context, was apparent. The relationship between the girl's ambition and her parents' expectations was also significant in determining her satisfaction with the sex role. Table-8 shows the approximate relative emphasis of the girls and their parents on academic achievement as reflected in the girls' responses.

Table-8

Girls' Perception of Degree of Emphasis on Academic Achievement.

Groups	*Emphasis by girls*	*Emphasis by parents*
Rural Lower SES	Low	Low
Rural Middle SES	High	Moderate
Urban Lower SES	Moderate	Low
Urban Middle SES	High	High
Urban Upper SES	Moderate	Moderate

While there was daughter-parent consonance in three groups (rural lower SES, urban middle SES and urban upper SES), it was found that when education was seen to be valued highly both by the girl and her parents the level of identification with the sex-role was low. A retrospective glance at the results will reveal that the actual levels of education were positively related with SES. However the need for academic achievement was not related in the same way. The emphasis was highest among the middle SES girls, moderate among the upper SES and lower SES urban girls and low among the lower SES rural girls.

The middle SES girl wanted to be educated so that she could find a job. Her education was probably seen by her parents as a means to improve her eligibility for marriage. In this social system the factor that can bring down the demand for dowry in marriage is the girl's education as it gives her the potential for employment. The girls themselves valued working outside the home to raise their income and status.

On the interpersonal front, the middle SES girls reported highly sex-differential practices among which the imposition of conventional curbs in socialisation was major. In short, they were expected to amalgamate a traditional low profile with a progressive working girl image. The dilemma of reconciling the opposing trends interfered in the process of defining a clear sex-role and hence of identifying with it.

6

Housework : Reality of the Gender Role

There was no doubt that girls, irrespective of SES level and place of dwelling, accepted housework as part of their life. With decreasing economic levels the participation of the girl in the household chores increased. Several subjects were actually doing more housework than their mothers. Although refusal to do household work was reported, it was resorted to as a means to express one's temper or to protest over something rather than as a protest against housework itself.

Table - 9

Contribution of Housework by Girls

	Rural		*Urban*			
	Lower SES	*Middle SES*	*Lower SES*	*Middle SES*	*Upper SES*	*Total*
Compared with other siblings subject worked	15	10	25	11	10	71
Brother expected to work at home	3	3	4	5	11	26

Note : Lower SES urban households were primarily nuclear with some mothers also going out to work.

As is evident from Table-9 in half the households adolescent girls had a major share in housework. There were no significant social class differences in this except with urban lower SES girls. The number of girls being primarily responsible for running the household was high in this case for perhaps two reasons. One, that these girls were capable of shopping and buying rations for the house, and so they did both outdoor and indoor housework. Secondly, since most families were nuclear and many mothers also went out to work, the responsibility of housework was not equally shared by other members, especially if the younger siblings were school-going.

In the upper SES urban sample, housework was not treated as a major responsibility. A large number said that work was shared almost equally among the siblings. The running of the house was mainly the mother's responsibility. The mothers did not expect their daughters to be able to run the house at that age, an expectation that middle and lower SES mothers did have. In the upper SES the mothers' expectation was that the girl would take her education seriously; and that once she was free from her studies she would learn domestic skills on her own.

7

Acceptance of Circumstances

There were two questions in the interview schedule that inadvertently revealed a great deal about the girls' acceptance of their gender and gender-role. These were :

- If someone asked you whether you wished to be a boy or a girl in your 'next birth', what would be your answer ?
- Are you happy or unhappy that you are a girl?

Table-10 shows the number of girls in different groups who said that they preferred to be born male or female in their 'next birth'. It also indicates the number of girls who expressed satisfaction/dissatisfaction with being female.

A comparative analysis of the results on the girls' satisfaction with their sexual identity revealed that the number of girls who were happy with their gender identity was lowest in the rural middle SES group and highest among the urban upper SES girls. However, there was not a predictable relationship between satisfaction with the present identity and preference for one sex or the other in the 'next birth'. The number of girls who wished to be reborn as males was highest in the rural middle SES and lowest in the rural lower SES group, which also had the highest number of girls who preferred to leave it to 'God' or 'Fate' to determine their gender instead of exercising a choice.

Table-10

Responses on Gender Preferred in 'Next birth' and Satisfaction with being Female.

	Rural		Urban			
Issues	*Lower SES*	*Middle SES*	*Lower SES*	*Middle SES*	*Upper SES*	*Total*
Gender in next birth:						
Male	9	25	18	17	14	83
Female	1	1	2	10	13	27
Undecided	6	1	2	3	3	15
God's will/fate	14	3	8	-	-	25
	30	30	30	30	30	150
Satisfaction with being female :						
No	13	19	15	11	7	65
Yes	12	3	11	15	20	61
Undecided	5	8	4	4	3	24
	30	30	30	30	30	30

On the response to this Hindu question there was no pattern. Although 61 girls said that they were satisfied with being female in 'this birth', only 27 were sure that they wished to be born female in the 'next birth'. There are two ways in which his finding can be perceived. One is related to the cultural heritage of children born in India. The Hindu view of life incorporates the concept of rebirth. The *atma* is seen as immortal which wears the garb of different mortal lives in successive births. It is of interest that none of the girls thought the question on rebirth to be odd. Within the culture this view is accepted without undue questioning.

In this context, the rural girls were found to be more traditional than urban girls. While conversing with them on the subject of 'next birth' the interviewer formed the impression that, on the whole, they considered rebirth as part of the cycle of life and death. They did not want to verbalise that which they did not want to happen, as if they attribute a magical power to mere verbalisation. In Anadalakshmy's words verbalisation in Indian culture is endowed with power and potency, as if merely talking about something would make it come true (1981, P.5). Hence, the girl's orientation towards her sex-role was reflected quite truthfully in her responses to the question on rebirth. The rural lower SES girls, being well-adjusted in their roles, preferred to appear uncertain as to what they wished to be, male or female, if another birth was granted to them. Only nine girls verbalised that they wished to be boys, while one girl did not want to be a girl again. The middle SES girls were largely unhappy in their sex-role as apparent through Table-10 and preferred to be born male.

The urban girls were significantly less traditional than the rural girls and on an average had more years of formal education. An unconfirmed and tentative hypothesis is that people who like to be seen as 'modern' and 'educated' try to dissociate themselves from traditional beliefs labelling them as 'old fashioned' or unscientific because their basis cannot be established rationally. Hence the middle and upper SES girls could well have treated the question of next birth lightly, perceiving it as traditional.

A second perspective on the lack of any trend in responses to the question on 'next birth' is as follows. Mere curiosity of experiencing the world of a male and not an unhappy present could have prompted some subjects to wish to be born male. There were cases of girls who said that they were happy being female in this birth, but would like to be born male in the 'next birth'. Very few girls had said that they were unhappy now and would still like to be born female.

It is relevant to suggest here that there is a cultural restraint against denouncing openly one's own life and circumstances as it connotes an insult to those who have brought one up and are a part of the immediate environment. Self-reproach also lowers one's self-esteem. Accepting reality as one's fate is socially more desirable. It is as though verbalising the fact that one is unhappy as a female now brings one face to face with reality, and if once articulated things would not change for the better. But transferring the need to the future is less guilt-producing as it does not cast aspersions on the present socialisers.

It can be surmised that all females who are well adjusted in their sex-role do not necessarily wish to be born female again and all the girls who prefer to be born male cannot be adjudged unhappy in the female role.

A question related to the issue of acceptance of identity asked much later under the subheading 'socialisation' was "Are you satisfied with your place in the family, responsibilities assigned to you and the circumstances of your family?" Table-11 presents the responses to this question.

Table-11
Responses of Subjects on Satisfaction with Present Circumstances

Yes/No		*Rural*		*Urban*			
		Lower SES	*Middle SES*	*Lower SES*	*Middle SES*	*Upper SES*	*Total*
yes	Because god given	5	1	-	-	-	6
	Acceptance	11	9	11	13	9	53
no		14	20	19	17	21	
	Economic inadequacy	6	4	9	2	1	22
	Personal reasons	10	19	14	15	20	78

Note : The sum is more than 150 as some subject gave more than one response.

Among the rural subjects, the lower SES girls who were unhappy with their circumstances mentioned poverty, lack of education and problems with in-laws as the reasons. On the previous question seven of these girls had also expressed unhappiness over being female. Among the middle SES girls dissatisfaction with life was widespread. Many subjects expressed their unhappiness over not having a brother or an older sibling. The inability to study further due to parents' unwillingness or lack of resources also led to frustration. Other factors such as reprimands at home, lack of independence, early marriage and preference for city life were also mentioned as causes of unhappiness.

In Delhi, poor economic condition was mentioned by some lower SES subjects as the reason for their dissatisfaction with their life. Most of the other girls mentioned lack of sufficient freedom as the major cause. The middle SES girls' reasons were more varied. Their personal reasons were low academic achievement, interference in working towards ambitions, lack of freedom and unemployment. Those related to the family and neighbourhood were low living standards, undesirable neighbourhood, lack of space and some family problems. It was apparent that a part of the causes of being unhappy was related to being female. Of the 17 girls who complained against their circumstances, 10 had expressed dissatisfaction with being female and 12 had wished to be born male in the 'next birth'.

The upper SES girls came out to be the most articulate in their expressions of differences with parents, but the factors were individualistic and intangible. Some examples in their own words are, "parents lay too much stress on studies"; "parents are more strict with me than with the older sisters"; "I wish I had a brother"; "parents are against inter-caste marriage"; "my parents don't get along"; "I want to work while my parents are not in favour of this" and "I'm not happy with my own life of education, i.e. medicine".

8

Menstruation : The Unmentionable Phenomenon

Findings concerning menarche were most unexpected and disturbing. There is a scarcity of documented evidence on the subject, specially in studies on northern India. However, an unofficial inside view would be that in the process of growing up, the girl would learn-purposefully or inadvertently, about menarche : what to expect and how to handle it. Contrary to the expectation, it appeared that there was no deliberate effort on the part of significant females around the girl to ensure that she was familiar with the process of menarche before it occurred. Table-12 presents data on their level of information regarding menarche.

The finding that more than 50 percent subjects reported not having had any knowledge about menstruation was in clear contrast to the studies done in the West which show that girls have definite knowledge of menarche before it occurs. In a study done in USA about beliefs concerning menstruation, the subjects not only included premenarcheal and post-menarcheal girls but also preadolescent boys (Clarke & Ruble, 1978). It was reported that all the three groups showed a high degree of awareness, suggesting that information on sexual development was readily accessible to boys and girls at a fairly young age.

In the present study those who reported having prior knowledge had obtained the information mainly through peers or through female family members other than mothers. Only in nine cases had the mother been the informant, eight of them being in the upper SES level.

Table-12

Responses of Girls on Questions Related to Menarche

Questions	*Rural*		*Urban*			*Total*
	Lower SES	*Middle SES*	*Lower SES*	*Middle SES*	*Upper SES*	
Knowledge about menarche prior to onset :						
No	20	16	16	18	8	78
Yes	10	14	14	12	22	72
Information received from :						
family members	-	3	2	3	11	19
peers	4	10	5	6	6	31
other means	6	1	2	3	4	16
Menstruation related to :						
reproductive function	9 (8 married)	7 (3 married)	7	10	26	59
overall growth	-	3	1	6	17	27
no idea	19	18	22	15	4	78

Not surprisingly, a large number of girls reported having been through unpleasant and embarrassing experiences at the time of menarche. However, this finding should not be taken to indicate that negative experiences of menarche had affected their perception of femininity negatively. Just as the traditional girl had shown a tendency to take things in her stride, she did not seem to harbour negative feelings about menstruation despite the unpleasantness she had faced at the time of menarche.

In general, it was one of the most difficult tasks to make the girls elaborate on their first menstruation. Many girls first said that their experience was normal. But when pressed further they revealed in a subdued and embarrassed tone, the nature of their experience. As in most other areas, urban upper SES girls were the least inhibited in their description. It was found that a negative experience was not always related to a negative perception of menstruation. In line with the low emphasis on the whole issue, there were practically no reports of girls feeling delighted at having commenced menstruation. In an American study of the emotional reactions of 475 girls to the onset of their menses, half of them reported their reaction as one of indifference, a significant minority being anxious or terrified. Only about 10 percent were curious or delighted (cited in Conger, 1977, P.122).

A significant correlate of ignorance concerning menarche and its relationship with the female reproductive function was the taboo attached to talking about the sexual aspect of life in general and to menstruation in particular. According to Ramanujam (1979), "We (Indians) seldom think about it (sex) without a sense of guilt. The ideal is abstinence or controlled sex towards the primary goal of procreation" (P.52).

Reporting on her data on urban Punjabis Das (1979) stated that among Punjabis the onset of menstruation was not announced publicly through ritual as done in many parts of southern India. She found that the women treated menstruation as a private matter and tried to keep it secret from the male members of the house. In other words the state of menstruation was never acknowledged publicly.

In the present study, among both the rural groups (one being from Punjab) and the three urban groups, no subject reported a ritual announcement of menarche in their family. Assuming that verbalising anything related to sex, except in hushed and embarrassed tones, was taboo, the girl was left to her own resources of discovering the reality before she attained puberty and to face the awkward situation. Some 'fortunate' ones, specially those living in large families, did have opportunities to observe older females or talk and joke with peers and find out about some facts of life. However, many of the girls had remained ignorant or hazy about menstruation until well after its onset.

An investigation of the girls' level of information about the significance of menarche in physiological development also revealed appalling results. Only a few girls, mostly urban, could relate it to fertility and bodily changes. Seventy eight girls could not say anything on the topic. In studies of urban samples Nangia (1981) and Pant (1981) also found a poor knowledge of female physiology among lower class girls. In the present study, among the educated girls also the information had been transmitted through peers and books. It was not delivered through the formal media of documentary films or classroom lessons or through socialisers like mothers and teachers.

The fact that the mother was conspicuously absent as an educator of the girl about menarche was an interesting finding. Several anthropological accounts and folk literature have depicted the mother-daughter relationship to be emotionally intimate (Cormack, 1961; Dube, 1967; Minturn & Lambert, 1964; Ross, 1962; Srinivas, 1952). According to Nandy and Kakar (1980) a "special kind of lenient affection and often compassionate attention (is) bestowed by mothers on their infant daughters throughout their lives" (P.147). It has been observed that the mother and the daughter overcome their interpersonal inhibition after the daughter gets married. This body of literature takes it for granted that the mother has the responsibility of ensuring that the daughter knows about the impending menarche either directly or indirectly.

Most probably, it was the cultural taboo against verbalising anything related to sex, specially between people of two different generations. The mother feigns indifference towards her daughter's maturity on the one hand and focusses on it on the other hand by increasing the supervision on her movements and conduct. The result is an impression of a lack of intimacy between the mother and the daughter, and the engendering of a temporary crisis for the daughter who feels cheated out of knowledge that could have been given to her. Almost all the girls in the study believed that the girl should be given this information well in time. While the urban girls felt that the mother was the most appropriate person to educate the girl, most rural girls felt that an elder sister or a *bhabhi* (sister-in-law) could do this job.

There is an Indianness to the phenomenon of not verbalising the most obvious of feelings and phenomena. In her paper on socialisation in India Anandalkshmy (1981) capsulises the picture in a sensitive comment, "While members of the family live in close proximity, their communication with each other about their feelings is minimal. Episodes and events are discussed at length, emotional tones are left to implication. There is affect and empathy and perhaps also antipathy but not articulation or analysis. Intimacy is hardly ever verbal". She further illustrates the point by quoting from a short story where the central figure is a 13-year-old girl. When the girl asks her mother, with whom she shares an affectionate relationship, "*Amma* (Mother), what is coming of age?" The mother retorts after a prolonged silence. "I want you to be just as you are now - romping around in your swirling skirts". In Anandalakshmy's words, "the mother thus throws away the perfect opportunity to prepare her daughter for menarche acting as though if she talked about it, it would become real, more real than reality itself."

The mother - daughter verbal gap despite emotional intimacy is characteristic of Indian culture. In contrast to this, the American mother is believed to convey some measures of information to her daughter prior to or at the time of menarche (Shopper, 1979).

In all the groups interviewed the woman was considered impure during menstruation. The observation of taboo regarding cooking, eating food, touching pickles or preserves and offering worship was commonly followed. Table 13 shows the distribution of responses on this.

Table-13

Restrictions Observed by Subjects During Menstruation
***N*=150**

	Rural		*Urban*			
Areas of Restriction	*Lower SES*	*Middle SES*	*Lower SES*	*Middle SES*	*Upper SES*	*Total*
Food/cooking	18	21	5	6	3	53
Entering place of worship	19	22	23	21	13	98
Total segregation	7 (5 married)	-	-	-	-	7

In the area of food, abstaining from handling pickle during menses was mentioned by many girls, as they believed that the preserve was likely to go bad if they touched it. While the restrictions were clearly observed by more rural than urban girls, it is possible that urban lower and middle SES girls did not practice these in relation to cooking, as the families were generally nuclear. If the women did not enter the kitchen or did not cook, the other members would starve. Hence the taboo of not cooking during menstruation was not being commonly observed so that it should not cause inconvenience to the men rather than because the woman was not regarded as impure. This is evident from the finding in the second area of restrictions. Not entering a place of worship, whether at home or outside, was a widespread practice; 98 out of 150 subjects reported this, including 13 upper SES subjects. These girls either believed in, or simply practised as a matter of habit, the notion that during menstruation they were 'impure' and hence should keep away from places of worship or objects linked with these, otherwise they would be committing a sin.

With increasing levels of education there was resentment towards these taboos, which were being observed to avoid a conflict in the family rather than because the girl was considered 'polluted'.

At the end of the analysis of the interviews there was a feeling that the casual manner in which menarche, a significant event in a woman's life, was treated revealed certain phenomena prevailing within the culture. It pointed to a low female status : menarche is for women and hence commands no attention. There seemed to be inhibition regarding sex to the extent of not acknowledging it as a positive and conscious need. This was related to the third characteristic of taboo against verbalising any topic concerned with sex. Menarche was a subject of embarrassment.

9

Marriage : The Undisputed Goal

Marriage was one area in which it had been both easy and difficult to interview the subjects. Easy because it is an event that assumes primary importance as a goal after the girl's puberty. The family's concern about the daughter's marriage is communicated to her through non-verbal cues, though nobody talks with her directly. Hence, it is assumed that she herself would be preoccupied with thoughts about her marriage and would be able to relate to its future possibility.

It became difficult too to probe deep into the issue of marriage, specially among the rural and lower class urban girls. These girls themselves perceived that they did not have the cultural sanction to participate in decision-making regarding their own marriage or articulate any preferences. Their code of conduct required them to be bashful about marriage. A delicate balance had to be maintained between the two. The cultural value for the girl being modest about her marriage has been reported by Jacobson and Wadley also (1977).

In the sample studied 22 girls were married and 8 were engaged to be married, as shown in Table 14.

Table-14

Number of Girls Married or Betrothed in Different SES Groups

	Rural		*Urban*			
Categories	*Lower*	*Middle*	*Lower*	*Middle*	*Upper*	*Total*
Married	10	4	6	-	-	20
Engaged	2	3	3	-	-	8

Most of the girls who were married believed that they had been married off too early by their parents. From their responses it was apparent that they had no role in deciding on their own marriage. They had not been consulted before the bride-groom was selected and most of them had not met him before marriage or engagement.

Table-15
Responses of Girls on Questions Related to their own Marriage/Engagement, *N*=28

Questions	*N = 12* *Lower SES Rural*	*N= 7* *Middle SES Rural*	*N=9* *Lower SES Urban*
Consulted before marriage/engagement -No	12	5	7
Husband Selected by :			
Parents	4	7	5
Other Relations	3	4	4
Seen husband before marriage/engagement :	4	3	2

The majority of the giris in the sample were unmarried while most of the rural girls and urban lower class girls anticipated marriage in the next one or two years, they did not consider it a subject about which they should know much or discuss. The reason can be seen in the responses that were received to some questions in Table-16.

Table-16
Responses of Unmarried Adolescent Girls on Issues Related to Marriage, *N*=122

	Rural		*Urban*			
Issues	*(18) Lower*	*(23) Middle*	*(21) Lower*	*(30) Middle*	*(30) Upper*	*Total*
1	2	3	4	5	6	7
1) Whether subject would be -Yes	3	2	7	5	29	46

(Contd.)

Table 16 (Contd.)

1	2	3	4	5	6	7
consulted about her marriage: -No	15	18	14	19	-	66
Not sure	-	3	-	6	1	10
2) Whether subject discusses marriages with others: -Yes	1	-	4	8	15	28
-No	17	23	15	21	15	91
No response	-	-	2	1	-	3
3) Choice of partner would be done by : -Self	-	-	-	2	6	8
Parents & Others	18	23	18	18	5	82
Mutually	-	-	3	8	19	30
No response	-	-	-	2	-	2
4) Dissatisfaction with parents' choice : Possible	4	11	14	26	29	84
Not Possible	9	8	5	1	-	23
Not desired	5	4	-	3	1	13
No response	-	-	2	-	-	2
5) Perceived control over own marriage : -No control	15	12	7	4	-	38
Little Control	3	8	11	13	7	42
Sufficient Control	-	2	1	10	23	36
No response	-	1	2	3	-	6

Conclusions regarding marriage were drawn on the basis of what was left unsaid or was half-said by a large cross-section of the sample (three groups). Only the urban middle and upper SES girls felt free to express their views and needs.

In the present study the level of education was positively related with the age at marriage and perceived control in marriage, and negatively related with the degree of inhibition in talking about marriage objectively. A semi-literate rural girl would respond in monosyllables and allow complete control over decisions about her marriage to her parents and other older family members. The educated urban upper SES girl, on the other hand, had faith in sufficient control over the factors related with her marriage and was willing to express her views openly. With decreasing traditionality level and increasing educational level, the view that girls should be consulted about their marriage was also found to be adopted more frequently.

One theme was constant at all levels of SES and education : the faith in parents' discretion to find a suitable match. The only difference was that the more traditional girls (supposedly belonging to traditional households) did not perceive the need to play an active role and regarded it as shameless to even ask questions about her marriage. The less traditional girls were inclined to see their non-participation as a limitation of the system. They wished that their opinion would be valued. However, the task of seeking a suitable match and arrange the marriage was left to the parents. Preference for a self-selected partners was also indicated by a few urban upper class girls. By and large marriage *per se* was not seen as a personal issue but as that concerning the whole family.

It was noteworthy that a large nubmer of urban (hence decreasingly less traditional) girls said that it was not necessary for women to get married, if they did not want to. Nevertheless, for themselves only a very small number of urban girls (seven out of 150) expressed the desire to remain unmarried. The reasons for this were not very clear.

10

Traditionality and the Adolescent Girl

The data on the Traditionality Scale, as seen in Figure 2, clearly showed that the rural girl was significantly more traditional than the urban girl. The rural lower SES girls scored the highest on 'traditionality' while the urban upper SES girls were the lowest on this variable. The rural middle, urban lower and urban middle SES girls were in between the two extreme levels in that order.

A break up of the mean scores of the subjects in the seven areas comprising the scale gives a picture of the relative contribution of scores through each area. Table 17 shows the mean scores of the subjects in each of the seven areas.

Table-17

Mean Scores of Subjects on Traditionality, $N = 150$

Group No.	*SES Group*	*Female Status*	*Family Loyalty*	*Caste*	*Discri-mina-tion*	*Fata-lism*	*Age hier-archy*	*Mar-riage*	*Total mean score*
1	2	3	4	5	6	7	8	9	10
I.	Lower (Rural)	6.13	5.73	5.80	5.10	6.97	6.57	8.87	45.16
II.	Middle (Rural)	3.83	5.80	4.43	3.93	3.90	5.43	6.73	34.06

(Contd.)

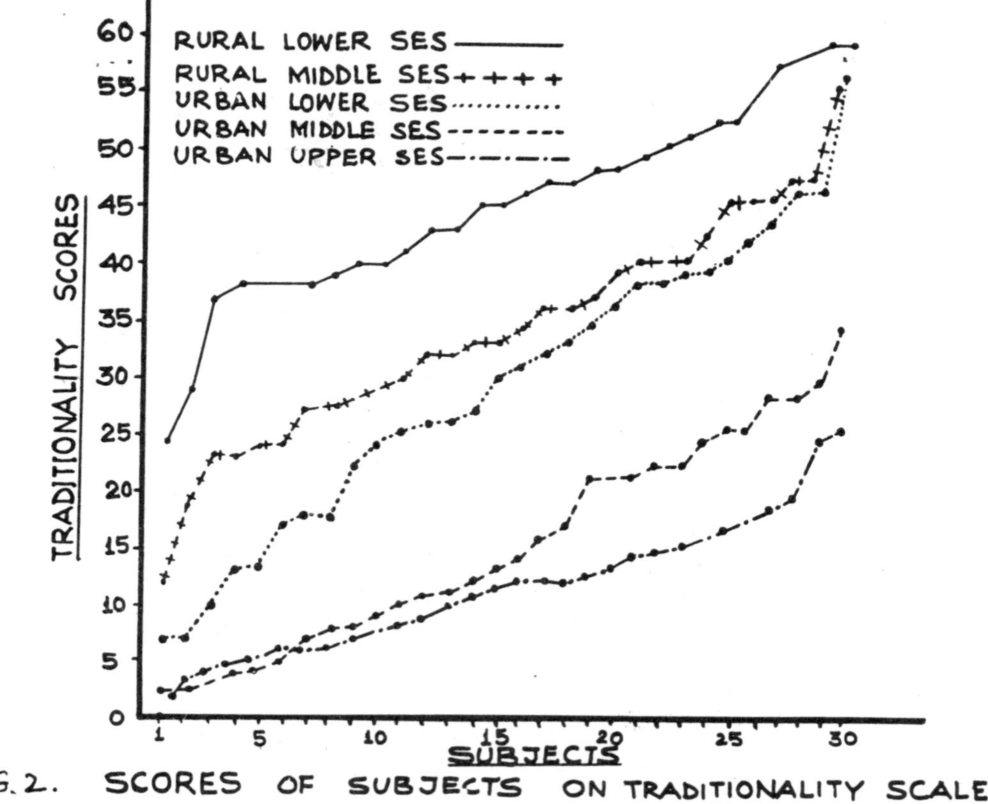

FIG. 2. SCORES OF SUBJECTS ON TRADITIONALITY SCALE

Table 17 (contd.)

1	2	3	4	5	6	7	8	9	10
III.	Lower (Urban)	3.63	4.53	3.00	2.87	3.53	5.00	6.63	29.20
IV.	Middle (Urban)	2.30	2.73	1.33	0.83	2.30	2.13	3.57	15.20
V.	Upper (Urban)	0.97	2.63	0.53	0.60	2.00	1.43	3.13	11.30
	Mean Score	16.85	21.42	15.09	13.33	18.70	20.56	28.93	

All the five groups have scored the highest in the area Marriage Customs. On Family Loyalty vs. Individualism also the scores are consistently, though not uniformly, high. The scores in the category, Discrimination between Sexes, are the lowest or close to that in all the groups. A comparative study of the cells of five groups in each of the seven areas indicates that not only are the cumulative mean scores arranged in a descending order from lower SES (rural) to upper SES (urban), but the mean scores in each area are also in that order (excepting the scores of lower SES (Rural) = 5.73 and middle SES (Rural) = 5.80 on Family Loyalty vs. Individualism.

This analysis suggests two findings. The proportion of traditionality being contributed through each of the seven areas towards overall traditionality level of the group is more or less equal in all the groups. Secondly, an even trend in directionality supports the validity of the scale as it orders the groups in one direction.

The analysis of variance revealed a significant difference between the five groups on traditionality, F (4,145) = 65.45, p.<.01. Table 18 gives a summary of the analysis of variance.

Table - 18

Effect of SES and Rural-Urban Residence on Traditionality of Lower, Middle and Upper SES subjects, *N* = 150

Source	*SS*	*MS*	*df*	*F*
1	2	3	4	5
Difference between groups	23116.04	5779.01	4	65.45*

(Contd.)

1	2	3	4	5
Difference within groups	12801.94	88.29	145	
Totals	35917.98		149	

*Significant at .01 level

These results indicate that within a given demographic set up (whether rural or urban) socio-economic status is negatively related with the level of traditionality. It also becomes evident that rural girls are significantly more traditional than urban girls irrespective of their SES.

Table - 19

Mean Traditionality Scores of Lower, Middle and Upper SES Subjects from Rural and Urban Areas.

Group No.	*SES Group*	*Mean*	*'t'*
I.	Lower (Rural)	45.16	16.56*
II.	Middle (Rural)	34.06	1.67**
III.	Lower (Urban)	29.20	4.91*
IV.	Middle(Urban)	15.20	2.15*
V.	Upper (Urban)	11.30	

*Significant at .01 level ** Significant at .05 level

The table shows that the differences between the mean scores of all the groups were significant, thus confirming the effect of SES and rural-urban background on the level of traditionality of the subjects.

In other words, being rural and lower class was associated with a high level of traditionality while being urban and upper class connoted a low level of traditionality. Any relationship between traditionality and sex-role identification then presupposes the interaction of these two demographic factors in the process.

11

The Adolescent Girl in the Socio-Cultural Context

Rural Lower SES

The girl from low socio-economic status living in a village was an adolescent only by virtue of her age, a criterion used to operationally define an adolescent. By all other standards she was an adult, having assumed adult responsibilities from the time she was a preadolescent. Housework as a major responsibility had started early for her, this being one of the reasons why most of the girls had discontinued schooling after primary education or had never been to school. The responsibility of child rearing had been handled by the girls from a young age. Early marriage, before or soon after menarche, had initiated many of them into the sexual functions of adulthood, which also brought early motherhood to some.

In addition to domestic responsibilities several young women also shouldered the task of earning a living for the family. Thus a girl who, at the age of 18 or 19 years, had been through several years of 'psychosocial adulthood' was generally found to be adult-like in her disposition.

A low level of socio-economic status in a rural area influenced the upbringing of the girl in many ways. In a situation of poverty, formal education of the girl was a luxury and the level of education of the average girl was very low. Moreover, she was also needed at home to help in managing a large family and was probably held back from school. However, it was convenient for the parents to tell her that it was appropriate for girls to get only a few years of formal education as that was socially acceptable. One of the subjects from Punjab, Lakhwinder, had to drop out of school when she was in the 5th standard. She said "Father's job was at a far off place and Mother was alone, so she said 'Don't study'. Then there were animals (buffaloes) at home to be looked after". Lakhwinder had three brothers, all of whom were learning carpentry.

Bhaini Devi enumerated a complexity of reasons for leaving school after the 5th standard. "I entered 6th standard but the family income could not sustain my education, and I also did not feel like continuing. My brother did not like my going to school. So I thought, 'If I have to leave tomorrow, I may as well leave today'. We were poor and it was difficult to make both ends meet. There was no fees in the school, but I was paying a token amount. Buying books, making the school uniforms, several other things have to be bought (when one goes to school) .... If you have to earn yourself to feed the family then where is the time for education?"

Consonant with and probably as a result of social expectations, the girls considered only a low level of education necessary. Those who were illiterate and employed as labourers often felt that having a few years of education would have enabled them to get jobs which did not involve manual labour. Bhagwati Bai was a construction labourer. According to her when as a child, she would go to school, her mother would bring her back and beat her if she talked again of going to school. Bhagwati was married into a family where everybody, including her husband, had some formal education. She said, "If I were also educated, I would not have been carrying bricks like this."

Among rural girls there was no stigma if a girl went out to work. They felt that formal education was a means to secure 'respectable' jobs. However, it was apparent that they did not anticipate such jobs for themselves as revealed by the absence of aspirations related to this. The unavailability of jobs other than manual would also have depressed their aspirations.

In families where the girl was not allowed to work outside, formal education of the girl seemed to be valued for its role in increasing her eligibility for marriage. In one family of U.P., where the subject (Kamla) was illiterate and 17 years old, the mother expressed anguish over her inability to find a match for her. The mother remarked, "These days if you talk of a girl's marriage, people ask 'What is her education?' When my daughter is not literate at all what answer can I give? (These days) nobody is less than 7th or 8th standard. If our daughter had also got some education it would have been good". Kamla herself lamented, "If one is educated, it is easy to pass one's time. If not more, they should have given me education upto 4th-5th standard. I could then write letters or read books.

Another correlate of low SES was a dichotomy between socialisation of girls and boys in the families. From the girls' responses about socialisation, it was apparent that the sphere of their activities was very limited. Those who worked outside to earn a living had moved out of the house as a necessity. But the others had to remain indoors. As against this the boys had no restrictions regarding their movements. They did no work within the house, nor were they expected to. Quite often it was the brother who imposed restrictions on his sister. For example, Gorja devi, 16 years of age, had a 13 year old brother who, she said, dominated over her. In her words, "He often says, 'where were you since the morning? You are always roaming around'. He also tells me 'So and so's daughter is bad, don't move about with so and so'.....He's younger than me, yet he can talk to me like this.... Yesterday I was late in coming back (from work) so he said, "Is this any time to come back? There are guests sitting at home, from where have you come?" He tells me, "You should be back from the fields before it is dark".

The lower class girls were aware of the favouritism shown to their brothers. Putting this metaphorically Rambai explained, "We are two sisters and a brother, He is indulged more. The girl is told, 'You go and work'. To the boy they (parents) say, "come child sit in the lap". Discrimination was also reported by others, one of them being Manbhavati, "My younger brother does not get scolded, but my mother abuses me. She also beats me. She says, 'Stay at home, Don't go out'. She also gives more food to my brother.

However, the girls had accepted the fact that they would have less freedom than boys. Quite often they did not approve of equal freedom to boys and girls, believing that girls were likely to go astray if given too much freedom. Manju, who was a young married woman, thought that it was inappropriate for girls to move about in the village. She said, "Constraints are essential for girls, not for boys. If boys get spoiled nobody laughs at them, but girls are laughed at. If anybody as much as looks at a girl, the girl's reputation is at stake. But nothing will happen to a boy's reputation even if a thousand people looked at him. After all he is a boy."

Kamlesh also reflected the general opinion of her group when she expressed approval of the restrictions on girls. "A grown up daughter has to be curbed. If she roams about people will talk about her. If you don't go to other people's houses then no one will know (that you are around). Boys' freedom is bound to increase while girls' freedom is bound to decrease. If you are a boy then it suits you to behave like a boy. If you are a girl it suits you to behave like a girl." The reputation of the family was also believed to be linked with the girls' conduct. Hadisa maintained, "The girl should be kept under check because what a girl does has influence on the prestige of the family members."

On principle the girls seemed to have internalised the differential treatment of sons and daughters in the family and had accepted the bias towards male children as the inevitable consequence of social circumstances. Pointing out the basis of this discrimination, Darshana, who was one of two daughters and five sons, stated, "Boys have to earn more; if the girls can't earn, it will do. Boys have more control over everything. It's their decisions that are carried out. Parents also tolerate the boys' wishes. Girls cannot do the same. They cannot show any preferences."

The girls believed that they were an economic burden on their parents. They supported the assumptions that sons looked after the parents in their old age and contributed towards family income while girls necessitated extra care and expenditure in their upbringing and they eventually left their parents after marriage. A construction labourer (Bhagwati Bai), who had two sons, said that she did not want to have a daughter as "it is burdensome" to bring up a girl.

The social interactions of the lower SES girls in rural areas were limited to those with the family members and relatives living in the village. Friendship with peers, who were not related to the family, was not permitted. A peer could be visited only if there was work and not just to talk with her. The subjects did not feel limited with regard to peer interactions since they did not consider it necessary to have a friends with whom they could share their confidences. This purpose was perhaps being served within the family through association with a sister, or a sister-in-law, or a cousin.

A number of reasons would account for these girls' attitudes of acceptance of the rules and their life events. A belief in the occurrence of what is 'written in their destiny' was expressed regarding marriage, family's economic condition and the future. Nearly half the group did not wish to exercise the hypothetical privilege of selecting one gender or the other for their "next birth" but left it to their fate to determine this. Not wanting to have specific aspirations, being contented with life despite their poverty, and believing events to be preordained were also indications of their faith in control by an 'external power', often referred to as God or Fate. For instance Kamlesh replied, when asked whether or not she was satisfied with her life, "Whatever has been ordained for us by God, we have to live it. So there is no question of not liking it".

Attributing a dominant role to a supernatural power was also a way of rationalising to themselves the lack of control over their lives; "When nothing can be done (by us) then I think that whichever way God makes us pass time is alright" were the words of Bhaini Devi. It may be granted that quite often the 'external power' was not an unknown factor but a person or a factor other than the girl herself. Thus if her brother or parents or her family's poverty had more control over her actions and destiny than she herself then these were external by definition. It was perhaps realistic and ego-adaptive that the girls did not consider themselves in control of their circumstances, since their lives appeared to be governed by a series of circumstances, the fact that they were women being one of them.

Family loyalty was reiterated through the support of the argument that curbs on a girl were necessary to protect her reputation which, in turn, was related to the family honour. The responses clearly showed that the girls generally obeyed their parents and other older relations. A girl who questioned parental authority was considered impertinent. Such a trait would also affect her eligibility for marriage, as she would be 'difficult' to get along with. Hence, wearing clothes according to the parents' wishes or not going out without parents' permission were not really signs of dependency on parents but requisites of obedient and modest behaviour.

Decisions regarding marriage, one of the most important events of their lives, lay almost entirely in the hands of their parents. The girls showed disinterest in discussing the topic of marriage. They were reticent and embarrassed in answering questions on marriage, especially if they were unmarried. They were socialised for this, since expressing interest in being married would be considered immodest. When questioned about their choices and preferences, the typical reply was, "there is no question of likes or dislikes. Whoever we are married to, we have to live with him, may he be blind or disabled"(Hadisa). Under such circumstances their feeling of lack of control over their marriage was understandable.

Apart from the implication that parents' decision on marriage had for the girls' character, it also highlighted the value for age and status. The girls accepted or were willing to accept their parents' and other older relations' choices in marriage. When Kamlesh was asked whether she would be consulted before her marriage was decided she replied, "No, it is not a practice in the village. When so many people are going to see the boy, then the girl's opinion is not going to be valued..... When everybody else likes the boy, then it is not possible to say 'no'."

An overview of the girls' perception of parental expectations regarding their conduct revealed that the rural girl was expected to maintain a very low profile. Bhaini Devi said that her parents' instructions were, "Don't move out much. When you go out don't talk or laugh too much. Don't answer back unnecessarily". These words could well be the instructions given to most of the girls.

The subjects themselves believed that a girl should not be seen or heard too much in the village. If she became a topic of discussion her reputation would be at stake. Narrating an example of what would be considered appropriate behaviour on the girls' part Rambai, who was very tall, said, "Suppose I am walking along and somebody jokingly says, "Hey! She's so tall', and then I also laugh back, it will be considered indecent. But if I pass by quietly then nobody will mind it."

The emphasis on the girl remaining almost invisible and unemotional in her reactions confirmed the attribution of a very low status to the female in a low SES set-up. Curbs on freedom of movement and speech also seemed to exercise a restrictive influence on her thoughts. The girls were rarely thinking about themselves. There was no evidence of introspection and 'thinking aloud' about their personal lives. Interestingly, the use of the expression "I" in Hindi or Punjabi was rare. Since individualism is not emphasized, talking about oneself would be considered self-centred behaviour and hence a negative personality trait.

This was perhaps also the reason why the girls were not able to verbalise their feelings and views about the kind of person they would like to marry and about other issues related to their marriage. It cannot be assumed that they were not thinking about the issues as marriage is made out to be the only acceptable goal in a girl's life. Practically all the subjects advocated marriage as an essential step in life though some of them perceived it as curtailing even the little freedom that they had before marriage.

There was a distinct absence of any deliberate communication to the girl about her impending maturational changes before they occurred. A low level of education coupled with the taboo of talking about matters related to sex appeared to result in an absence of information about menarche and feminine development. There seemed to be a lack of intimacy between the mother and the daughter as indicated by the inadequacy of verbal communication between them. The mother did not prepare her daughter for menarche or marriage, leaving it to incidental learning, observation or personal experience. Older sisters or sisters-in-law sometimes acted as confidants.

The responses related to menarche strengthen the argument that the girls were not used to thinking or talking about themselves. They found it hard to verbalise their experience of menarche, partly because of its sexual connotations. If the biological changes had affected these girls' personality in any way, the interview method was not adequate in investigating it. Their responses were usually sketchy and unemotional. One of the more articulate subjects Rambai, who was married, narrated her experience of menarche, "I showed my Tai (Aunt) that I had some stain on my clothes. When she saw it she exclaimed, 'Ram Ram get away! Wash your clothes and sit away from everybody'. Then I held my head in my hands and cried, 'What is this happening?"

The girl's womanhood became a stigma for her and a symbol of lower status because of the taboos attached to the purely biological function of menstruation. Describing an extreme form of segregation during menstruation Gauri, who was also married said, "I cannot cook for six days. My husband makes the food and hands it over from a distance. I cannot touch water, the cow, the cowshed or cowdung". In general, the restrictions on girls during their monthly periods were not so extreme, but the practices were sufficiently noticeable to demarcate them as 'polluted'.

It can be envisaged that the misfortune of being born a female becomes apparent to the girl quite early in her life although she identifies with her social role quite adequately. However, role identity is not parallel to ego-identity achieved after a period of crisis and active questioning regarding selfsameness. Following the Eriksonian model of identity formation, the girl from the lower SES lacked on ego identity, but had a social identity; one girl could be more or less prototype of all the other girls in the rural group.

Case Profile

Nankai

Nankai was located through a middle SES subject Manju, in whose house Nankai's mother worked as a part time servant. Before Nankai was finally interviewed, Manju had to plead with her to cooperate. Nankai did not seem to be averse to conversing with a 'stranger'. Rather she was extremely shy to be interviewed by an 'upper status' person, the purpose of the interview being beyond her comprehension. When Nankai arrived at Manju's house for the interview her face was covered by a *purdah* and she giggled at every query.

It was decided not to interview her at her own house as Manju informed the investigator that her married brothers did not have congenial relations with Nankai, and her mother and therefore, might pose problems in the interview.

One reason for Nankai's repeated efforts to cover her face was that she had been married for only 2 1/2 months and newly married girls in a village are expected to observe modesty. Nankai's '*gauna*'* took place along with her marriage. At the time of interview she was visiting her native village for a few days for the first time after her marriage.

Nankai's family belonged to a scheduled caste. Her father had died when she was quite young. The youngest child among seven, with three brothers and three sisters, Nankai had never been to school. All her siblings were also married. The brothers had separated their kitchens from the mother's kitchen, although they shared the same courtyard. Before her marriage, Nankai had worked as a domestic servant along with her mother. Even during her temporary stay in her natal home she was assisting her sickly mother in her work outside the house.

Being forbidden to move about in the village was not seen by Nanaki as a discriminatory practice. She felt that she had not seen any bias in favour of her brothers in her family. Yet the fact that there were differences, which she might not have seen as unfair, was indicated by her wish to be a boy in her 'next birth'. She said that she could then do whatever she felt like, implying that boys were allowed more freedom than girls.

There was nothing unusual about the fact that Nankai was married at the age of 16. However, the circumstances in which Nankai got married appeared to be somewhat surprising, if not dramatic. The story was narrated by Manju in Nankai's presence who nodded her consent throughout. Nankai's husband had been earlier engaged to another girl from some other village. But their engagement was called off as the girl's relatives believed a rumour that the young man was deaf and mute.

The bridegroom's family had already sent off invitations for the wedding. Hence, to save themselves from embarrassment, they fer-

* In India, when girls are married early, that is, before or just after puberty, they are sometimes not sent to their husband's home immediately. When they finally leaves for their husband's home the event is referred to as "gauna".

vently searched for another bride. A common acquaintance suggested Nankai to them as the prospective bride. She was viewed and found suitable and the wedding took place within days of the meeting. According to Nanaki, due to the hurry and also because her brothers did not contribute anything towards the wedding, she received only a *Thali*,* a *Katori*,** a spoon and a purse as dowry from her mother. She said that she had not been teased or taunted by her in laws for taking such a small dowry.

It was possible to discern a feeling of satisfaction in Nanaki's responses about her marriage, despite her inhibition to elaborate on anything. With a mischievous smile she said that she had not found her husband to be dumb, as feared by many. He had studied upto high school and was working on the family farm.

Nankai identified with her sex role quite adequately. She agreed that her marriage had taken place at the right time, she expressed approval of her husband saying "How can a girl say anything?" She would have accepted her hurried marriage to a possibly handicapped person as a stroke of fate, realising that her mother was extremely poor and would find it hard to seek a match for her without any support from her sons.

Nankai viewed living with her husband's parents as a natural consequence of marriage and she valued living in a joint family. Of course she admitted that she had to observe many more restrictions at her husband's house compared to those in her own village. Thus, she had to be in *purdah*, she could not leave the house even to fetch water and was not allowed to stand at the front door. Her one complaint was "I don't feel settled yet".

Another indicator of acceptance of restrictions was that Nanaki willingly observed many taboos during menstruation. She said she had no knowledge about the relationship between the menstrual cycle and pregnancy.

Several conclusions seem to emerge from the study of Nankai's profile. It was apparent that a girl from a low caste and a low economic status was powerless in most decisions of her life. Nankai's marriage

---

* a metal plate.

** a metal bowl

had been contracted taking her consent for granted, even though there was the risk of the bridegroom being handicapped. Considering the fact that Nanki was illiterate and poor while her husband was educated and a small scale farmer, it was possible that he had some speech defect. If Nankai did not reveal this in the interview she was simply being a traditional wife who accepts her husband with all his defects and would never let any criticism of him enter her conversation with others.

Nankai's case also revealed the amount of ignorance prevailing about sexual development. Not only had Nankai been left to go through menarche without anybody giving her any information, even after marriage she had no knowledge about the procreative aspect of menstruation. It may be naive to assume that what was not verbalised, was also not known. Nevertheless the taboo associated with sex was strong and Nankai was silent on the function of the menstrual cycle.

Rural Middle SES

"I get up in the morning, attend to my morning ablutions, and then milk the buffalo. Then I clean up the kitchen and make tea. I make the dough and bake chapatis for my brothers. Then they go away on their work. After that I scrub the utensils and clean up the place. When I am free from this work I sit down to embroider a shawl". In these words Jagir Kaur of a Punjab village narrated the routines of her daily life. She also depicted an approximately representative picture of the heavy routine of a rural middle SES non-school going girl. The school-going girls had less housework to do.

The moderately educated middle SES girl was performing the traditional role expected of an adolescent daughter or a daughter-in-law, as the case may be. She accepted household responsibilities as part of her life. But she was not satisfied with doing only housework. She wanted freedom to occupy herself during her leisure. She also felt that her parents should have more faith in her. Nisha, who had completed Intermediate, was unhappy about the restriction on her to go and see a film specially when her brother could go. She remarked, "Educated girls mind such things more. Girls who are not educated would not mind it so much if they are not allowed to go and see a movie".

The adolescent girl in a rural middle class family was found to have a life pattern quite similar to that of her lower SES counterpart. However, she differed from the latter in that her level of education was higher and she was inclined to express her opinions more freely than the lower SES girl.

Certain characteristics of the group emerged that could be related to the formal education of the girls. The need for autonomy was discerned in many instances. The girls wished to have education upto high school or more. The need for a higher level of education was usually coupled with the aspiration to have a job. Kusum, who had studied upto Intermediate, had wanted to study more so that she could become a teacher or a typist. She felt that "An earning girl can become independent, she can stand on her own feet."

It was observed that education was usually not perceived as an end but as a means to achieve several goals. Schooling was seen to bring status, to provide eligibility for a job, and to improve qualifications for a good marriage. Although dowry demands were said to increase if educated bridegrooms were sought, in some cases a few years in school compensated partly for the dowry. Rekha maintained, "If the girl is not educated, then the dowry has to be given. If she is educated, then perhaps a little less can be given. She can find a good family also. Educated girls are more in demand. It is said, 'The girl is educated; if there is no dowry, it is alright'."

Undoubtedly, this perception was wishful thinking rather than a reality. But implicit to this kind of thought is the acceptance that an educated girl could exercise some control over her marriage and might refuse to marry into a family which demanded a large dowry. An alternative assumption could be that an educated girl would be sought by families who valued having an enlightened daughter-in-law. Such people would themselves be 'educated', though not necessarily formally, and would not treat dowry as the main factor determining the girl's suitability for marriage.

In all these families, the male was seen to be more privileged than the female. Twenty five girls wished to be born males in their 'next birth', the largest number among all the five groups of the sample. Satisfaction with being a girl was very low (3). The girls perceived their brothers as irresponsible; boys were not given any work in the house as it was not considered their responsibility. The subjects felt that their parents were lenient with their brothers and hence they had become 'spoilt'. Nisha did not have a mother and she was the only unmarried girl in the house with two younger brothers. She complained, "My brother does not do any work in the house. If he is in a good mood he fills up water (from the well) otherwise he does not even do that. If I say anything to him he does not listen, so there is no use saying anything. He sometimes attends to errands outside. There is no one to scold him and he does not listen to me or *Baba** and *Dadi.***"

A brother's right to control his sister was also resented by the girls. Jagir Kaur commented, "A brother may beat his sisters but they won't even lift their hand". Talking about her own brothers she said, "They go away to the city and see films etc. But If I go to a friend's house they say, 'What do you go for from house to house, can't you sit in the house and work?' If I say 'I had gone to Rano's or Kuldip's house to embroider the shawl', they tell me 'Can't you embroider your shawl at home'?"

The girls were envious of the male privileges and prerogatives such as fewer curbs, opportunity for higher education, living with parents after marriage, the absence of the menstrual cycle and their importance as sons. They were thus critical of their own role and resented being female. Sudha Rani, who was married, had studied upto 8th standard. She conveyed her experience of being female in these words. She said, "I would like to be a boy (in the next birth) because womanhood is bad. Wherever she (a woman) stands, she will earn a bad reputation. If she talks to anyone then also .... I would like to be a boy. You can do whatever you like, nobody is going to say anything. If somebody turns me into a boy right now I'd be willing .... A boy can be of great service to his parents. Girls can only cook. They cannot earn or do any such thing."

The attribution of life events to a supernatural power such as God or Fate was not very common in this group. But at the same time the girls felt powerless and frustrated. Most of them were able to verbalise the reasons for their disillusionment with life. The central core under-

---

* Grandfather

** Grandmother

lying most of their complaints seemed to be their gender. Expressing disenchantment with her life as a female, Rekha said, "Whatever God makes one, one has to be .... who likes to be at home (all the time)? One feels suffocated sitting at home day and night." Rekha had studied upto 8th standard and for further education she would have had to go to the city, which her parents did not allow.

Another characteristic of the rural middle SES group was a certain amount of uncertainty that surrounded the issue of marriage. While most of the girls did not anticipate marriage in the next 2 years - some of them expecting it only 3-4 years later - it was most likely that they would be married off soon. Those who were continuing education, could postpone marriage until their education was over. But those who had discontinued seemed to be unwilling to be married yet, though they felt that they had no valid excuse to shift the time of marriage forward if a proposal was accepted by the parents.

Yet marriage was very much a part of the girls' perception of their immediate future. Some of them were engaged in embroidering sheets and pillow covers for their dowry. Some others inadvertently made statements which revealed their anxiety regarding marriage. For example, Anjana Kumari, who was studying in 9th standard and had two sisters and two brothers younger than her said, "It would have been better if we had an elder brother. He would have earned to make dowry for the sisters."

There seemed to be some conflict in the girls' minds. They were living in a system where a girl's marriage was contracted without seeking her opinion, taking her consent for granted. The girls, however, indicated that it was only fair that they should be asked whether or not they were prepared to get married and whether they had any opinion about the young man selected. A dissonance between their needs and reality was obvious.

It was apparent that the girls had internalised the social norm that the woman is less important than the man. Nearly one-third of the sample held the opinion that formal education was less important for girls than for boys. Most of them did not demand more freedom of movement although they felt very restricted in their environment. One subject reported (Ruchi Bharati), "There is a restriction on my going out. I cannot go to anybody's house. I can only go to school when the school is open. My brothers go out anywhere. If they come back late from school they say, 'We were having classes until late today'. Having too many friends or moving about in the village were considered as traits of an immodest girl. They also felt that the observance of taboos during menstruation was necessary although it was embarrassing to them.

The identity of the rural girl centred around her acceptance in the community. Social acceptance of the girl seemed to be of prime importance to the parents. They laid down rigid strictures and were not willing to tolerate any behaviour that might elicit social disapproval. Academic achievement was not considered by the parents as a quality that would improve the girl's image. In fact 'too much' education was expected to affect the girl's acceptability negatively. Summing up the expectations of most parents regarding correct behaviour: Rani descibed her parents' injunctions, "You are a girl, you must follow the correct path. Never tell a lie. Stay within limits. Don't be fashionable before marriage. Look after your reputation, it should not bring dishonour to us. We should not have to hear anything negative about you from others".

While discussing the types of restrictions imposed on her, Jagiro complained, "If you comb your hair or put *Surma** they say, 'why have you put it'? If you wear new clothes they will say, 'why are you so coquettish; how she dresses up and moves around'!" Indicating to the girl that her parents' house was not her own and she should be restrained before marriage, Lakhwinder's parents would tell her, "When you go to your 'own' house do whatever you want to, not at your parents' house". They did not allow her to wear expensive clothes. The middle SES girls often wore clothes of their parents' choice. The school-going girls had some control over the type of clothes they selected for themselves, but the range of variation was extremely limited.

Instructions to a married girl were different. Sudha Rani narrated the lessons given to her by her parents, "Devote yourself in the service of your parents-in-law and husband. Obey the elders. Whatever your in-laws say, it is right. You are young, you may not like it. They will say, *Bahu*** don't go out,' you will mind it. But they are right if

* A Hindi word meaning powdered eye blackening.

** Daughter-in-law.

they say this." The cultural value for respect for age and status is explicit in these words of wisdom, which allow no scope for the girl's individual wish or discretion coming in the way of service and obedience.

Fear of social disapproval seemed to monitor the girl's behaviour significantly. There were unwritten norms about every move that a girl could make. Thus she did not move out of the house and wore only modest clothing of the kind that was socially sanctioned. She could not seek employment and had to be married at the 'right' age. Deviation from these norms would invite criticism from the neighbours and relatives, and sometimes the whole community. Echoing this observation, Meena said, "If not married, others will think, 'What is the reason for her not getting married?' The girl also thinks that if she does not get married other people will laugh at her (saying) 'She's not married yet; wonder what the reason is?"

The mother was not perceived as a confidante. The only reference made to the mother by the girls was as a disciplinarian. It is possible that she was seen in this role more prominently because the girls were just past their menarche and the restrictions on them would have increased. Both the mothers and the daughters appeared to find it awkward to talk about menarche or marriage. In other words, the girls went through these critical phases of life without being instructed in any way. While in an urban set up, educated girls can read or hear about these subjects, in a rural area these avenues are closed. It would normally be expected that there would be hidden channels of information in a culture where verbalising openly on the theme is disapproved.

However, it could be assumed that either such channels were not in operation or there was a stigma attached to an unmarried girl having knowledge about sexual development. Perhaps she could not admit to having such information. In such a situation it was understandable that the girl did not know the relationship of menarche to pregnancy and childbirth.

In sum, the middle SES rural girl emerged as a young person who aspired for some freedom to experiment with different roles, while she was actually expected to perform a narrowly defined role. Her experience of formal education seemed to have a significant role in increasing her awareness of opportunities for self-enhancement. However, the incompatibility of the values projected by the modern system of education with the socio-cultural milieu of the village became apparent.

The data revealed that the middle SES rural girl was, on the one hand, socialised to lead a restricted and protected life. On the other hand, her formal education had enabled her to think a little freely and to seek slightly different goals than those sought by the women of her mother's generation. She considered herself potentially superior to the illiterate girl. She questioned the restrictions imposed on the girl, contrasting them with the freedom of the boy. She envied the male for his prerogatives and status and wanted to simulate his life.

The rural girl's obedience to authority, if she was a middle SES girl, was more out of lack of choice rather than due to unquestioning acceptance of authority. She wanted to be economically productive (e.g. have a job) since that was one way of redeeming her status. She desired marriage at an older age, which was also a sign of her need to prolong her adolescence. Her wish to exercise more control over her own life was guided by her orientation to a predominantly internal locus of control.

It appeared that the middle SES rural adolescent girl was not well identified with her socially determined gender role. In fact, the overall picture was that of a person with a sense of impotence.

Case Profile

Kusum Nigam

Kusum was the first subject that the investigator interviewed in the U.P. village, Ismail Ganj. An informant who lived in that village introduced the investigator to Kusum's *Tauji** on their first visit to the village. The old man was literate and seemed to understand the meaning of the term research. He agreed to allow three of his adolescent nieces to be interviewed for the study, Kusum being the eldest of them.

* Father's elder brother.

Kusum's house had several rooms and a courtyard. Some portion of the house was *pucca** and some portion was *kucha***. The sitting room had only four chairs and was sparsely furnished. Against one wall of this room, a motorised bicycle was parked. Kusum said that her father normally drove it but it was out of order.

Kusum's father was a clerk at the Secretariat in Lucknow. He had B.A. and L.L.B. degrees. Her *Tauji*, who was a bachelor, owned a small grocery shop in an outer room of the house. He wielded a lot of control over the family, perhaps more than his brother and he supervised the activities of the girls from his shop.

At 19 years, Kusum had three sisters and two brothers younger than her, the boys being the youngest. She had completed her Intermediate and had been out of college for two years at the time of interview. She had had her high school and Intermediate education at Lucknow.

Kusum had wanted to do a B.A. degree and become a teacher or a typist but her family did not favour this. *Tauji* had not allowed her to take up a teacher's job even in the middle school within the village, a fact which had upset Kusum. She elaborated her family's reasons for not allowing her to work outside as, "They think that grown up girls should not go out, because people in the society will laugh and say, 'the parents are living on the girl's income'." Kusum felt that she might have been able to convince her parents to allow her to go for higher education, but not *Tauji*. He, she said, was very old fashioned regarding girls' conduct.

The housework was attended to by all the girls, though Kusum had more responsibilities than others. About her mother's role she said, "She only orders us about, 'You do this and you do that'." It became apparent that doing housework was not enough for Kusum. She said that she had become disillusioned with life because she felt powerless in the face of the authority of the older people. She lamented, "I am unhappy because my education is incomplete. Secondly, our standard of living is not of the level I desire. I have tried to work towards this but have been unsuccessful. The worst thing is that what I wish is not considered important. The elders in the house assert themselves and do not

* Made of cement and bricks.

** Made from mud and cowdung.

listen to us. Here nothing moves without the approval of elders." Kusum also regretted the fact that members of the older generation were always finding fault with them (the girls) and did not appreciate the fact that they were educated and wanted to achieve something in life.

An incident that occurred in the course of data collection in the village would illustrate the degree of constraint on girls in general and Kusum in particular. When the investigator wished to be introduced to more adolescent girls for interview, Kusum said that she knew of many girls in her neighbourhood, but she would not be able to accompany the investigator to their houses. The reason given by her was that she was not allowed to move out of her house without a sound reason. She did not think that helping a stranger locate houses in the village would be considered a sound enough reason, specially since the other girls were not relatives of her family.

There was one young woman, to whose house she promised to accompany the investigator provided *Tauji* was not at home. So one day when this opportunity arrived, Kusum informed her mother, covered her head and led the investigator to her friend's house.

Kusum was more knowledgeable than most of her peers about menarche and its significance. But she admitted that she would not be able to answer questions about it frankly, thus reflecting the cultural reticence in discussing matters related to bodily functions. Kusum did not approve of taboos related to menstruation. She was also critical of the restrictions placed on the girl after she attained menarche. She commented, "They (the parents) would not let us talk to or meet any-one.... They won't let us sit among men. Even if a boy is a cousin, we won't be allowed to be with him. These things bother us."

Kusum did not seem to be looking forward to marriage. She believed that it was not essential for every woman to get married. According to her if a woman could earn well and support herself, she could choose to remain unmarried. About her own marriage she talked differently, as though it did not matter when and to whom she was married, as she did not expect to play a major role in the decision. When asked whether she had thought of any specific qualities that she would like in her husband, Kusum mentioned a few and added, "He should be like me, not very handsome - because I am ugly."

The investigator's observation was that Kusum had a fairly pleasant disposition, though she lacked conventional good looks. It is possible that she had been rejected by many parties due to her lack of good looks, (her complexion was not fair!) and she herself might have rejected some offers of less educated candidates. According to Kusum, her parents had been on the look out for a son-in-law from the time she was in high school. Perhaps, by their standards, her marriage had already been delayed. These factors could have contributed to her indifference and a feeling of powerlessness.

Despite her feeling that she was caged in her surroundings, Kusum did not express a wish to be born a boy in her 'next birth'. Her opinion was, "If I can have freedom as a girl, then I have no wish to be a boy .... In this birth also I want to have more freedom, I don't wish to be a boy."

Kusum's conflict was more visible than that of the average middle SES rural girl. However, her case supported the general observation that the adolescent girl in this group valued an individual identity as against the 'collective' identity that she was expected to take. Kusum's resistance of age-old stereotypes and open denunciation of the socially expected female role was perhaps a result of her being educated and having more choices than the illiterate or the less educated girl.

Urban Lower SES

The data on urban lower SES adolescent girls revealed that a single profile of a typical working class girl did not emerge. There were considerable intra-group differences. To some extent these differences could be attributed to factors such as varied levels of education of the girls, their marital status and male-female ratio in the family. However, some general features also emerged that were characteristic of a majority of the girls in this group.

Value for formal education seemed to find an important place in the value-system of these girls. Given the chance, all except two girls would have completed their education up to high school level. They perceived education as a means to achieve a life of less manual work, greater comfort and prestige. Being able to read and write and keep accounts seemed to be valued to reduce dependency on others and achieve some control over the future. Formal education was also treated as a passport to finding a well-to-do and educated husband. Vocational aspirations, though present even among the less educated, were higher among the more educated. The employment of a girl was seen to enhance her status and prestige.

Mansa was working as a part-time servant. She had education upto 3rd standard. She indicated that she did not like doing that kind of work. In her words, "A job that is taken up on the basis of educational qualification brings prestige."

The data showed that when a lower-class girl goes to school, she does so against odds like responsibility for younger siblings, housework, and lack of space and privacy. When the family cannot afford formal education, it is the girl who has to drop out from school. When the mother needs an extra hand in the house, the girl is held back from school. These were the reasons for many of the subjects in this sample having discontinued their education.

Working to supplement family income was common. A girl who worked as a part time servant usually had no education or only a low level of it, say upto 5th standard. She visited several houses in a day either alone or with her mother or sister and cleaned utensils etc. Four out of five such girls were attending a free tailoring class to learn sewing. This was the only time when they could sit and chat with their peers.

Peer interactions were, however, few and generally discouraged by parents. Talking to another girl or visiting a friend without any specific reason was not permitted. Girls were constantly reminded to stay indoors and to mind their own business. They were allowed to visit the houses of only a few known families in the neighbourhood and were discouraged from having more than one or two friends. Often girls reported to having no friends at all. Talking to an unfamiliar boy or man was prohibited after a girl had attained menarche.

Differences in the socialisation of boys and girls were quite apparent in the lower SES families. The major aspect of differentiation that irked the girls was the greater freedom of physical movement given to boys. Indulgence towards boys was coupled with extra restrictions on girls, and almost half of the girls resented this fact. They envied their brothers their greater freedom and fewer responsibilities. Jaswinder wished to be born a boy in her next birth. Her main reason was that she received constant reprimands from her brothers and her mother. "When I get scolded, I say, 'God, why did you make me a girl! It would have been good if you had made me a boy'. Boys are not scolded. They may come home any time from anywhere, but there is no question of asking them where they had been."

If a boy was late in coming home, parents did not take much notice, but if a girl was slightly delayed it caused great worry and raised tempers in the family. Not being able to move about freely in the neighbourhood, let alone beyond, was seen by the girls as a major drawback of being a girl. Pushpa Tiwari was a trained *Balsevika.** However, she was not allowed to go to work as the *Balwadi*** where she was offered the job was several miles away from her house. Pushpa remarked, "Being a female I would not be sent so far off. If I were a boy, they would have sent me even if I had to go out of Delhi." However, nearly half the subjects accepted the restrictions placed on them as necessary and justified because, in their view, a girl's prestige in society was more vulnerable than a boy's.

The discrimination between sexes in socialisation was probably a crucial factor in determining the girls' degree of satisfaction or dissatisfaction in their roles as females. A majority did not wish to be born female again. They did not resent housework, or marriage or the prospect of bearing children as much as the physical and social limitations associated with being a female. It is the desire to be able to do what a boy was allowed rather than a negation of what girls have to do that perhaps was responsible for their preference for being male in the 'next birth'. The superior status of the male in the society was not mentioned *per se*, but the privileges they enjoyed. Girls who experienced many more restrictions compared to their brothers were those who resented the bias in favour of the male.

---

* A child-welfare worker.

** A child-welfare centre for children between 3-6 years to provide health, education and nutrition facilities

Some daughters were, nevertheless, also indulged by the family, especially if they were the youngest. Restrictions were enforced less strictly on them and the girls themselves perceived having a fair amount of freedom in the family.

The father rarely figured in the girls' conversation as an active disciplinarian. The girl's mother or brothers were the main supervisors of her conduct. A physical and emotional distance from the father was maintained, but his instructions regarding behavior were followed unquestioningly. If any concessions were sought or opinions were expressed by the girls, these were conveyed to him through the mother. As an exception to this pattern, attachment to the father emerged in the conversations of four girls. One of them, an only child, had no mother and had been brought up by the father from an early age. In the other three cases, the mother was exacting and punitive towards the daughter. The father seemed to take sides with the daughter at the time of mother-daughter conflicts and was perceived as being more nurturant than the mother.

Disobedience or defiance was generally not reported because the subjects themselves did not approve of such conduct for girls. A few reported being reprimanded or physically punished by the mother for disobedience.

The interview data of the lower SES girls revealed that mothers and daughters communicated very little with each other on a personal level. They spent most of the time together and the daughter received her training directly from the mother. However, there was no emotional intimacy wherein individuals overcome their hierarchical boundaries and talk about personal problems and experiences. Girls were reticent and could not imagine talking to their mothers about their own marriage. Another indicator of restraint in the relationship was that many girls had entered menarche without being told by anyone about it, so that most of them had negative experiences. As an illustration Ramwati's case would be interesting. She had been married at the age of 11 years. However, her *gauna* had not been performed. She had no knowledge about menarche beforehand and hence had an unpleasant experience the first time the periods occurred, "I cried a lot (when it happened). Mother did not know why I was crying so much. I did not tell her.... If a mother talks about this it becomes very embarrassing, she will also feel awkward."

After menarche, the girls seemed to reduce their interactions outside the home. Alongside, the search for a suitable partner for marriage was intensified, specially if there were no unmarried older sisters. If not attending school, they were expected to devote most of their time to housework.

Girls were considered marriageable from puberty onwards, with the exact age of marriage depending on factors such as the number of daughters, the economic condition of the family, value of education for the girl and availability of a suitable match. If married in the early teens, the *gauna* was not performed until a few years later. The girl's consent carried little value, though a higher level of formal education seemed to delay the age of marriage. The subjects anticipated no control over the selection of their marriage partner, time of marriage and other details related to their own marriage. They accepted their exclusion from this domain with shy complacency and a view that parents knew better than they did. Their perception of a good husband was that of someone who did not drink or gamble and had a regular, salaried job.

None of the girls approved of marriage before 18 years and even those who were married thought they had been married too early. Marriage was considered essential by most girls, although there were a few (9) who did not think so. Living with the joint family was regarded as a natural arrangement after marriage. Only a few anticipated setting up a separate household if disharmony between the two generations prevailed.

In conclusion, it can be inferred that a lower SES urban girl grows up exposed to several hypothetical choices which are not real for her because of the control exercised by others. She has only a few opportunities, such as formal education to enhance her own self. The development of a sense of ego identity is clouded by social identity she acquires when governed by limitations and taboos related to formal education, freedom of movement, peer interactions, the menstrual cycle and marriage. There were signs of an urge to achieve some independence from customary limitations. However, there was no identity confusion, as the girls seemed fairly identified with their social roles.

Case Profile

Shakuntala

Shakuntala was 18 years old, eager to learn and keen to be interviewed. Her father and elder brothers were sweepers with the New Delhi Municipal Corporation and the family lived in a two room tenement in Bapu Dham, a colony for class IV employees of NDMC. Second in birth order of a family of seven children, Shakuntala had five brothers and one sister. The elder brother was married and his wife and two children were also living with them. In all there were 12 members in the family.

Shakuntala had not received any formal education although all her younger siblings were going to school. She had to shoulder the responsibility of the care of younger children and household chores from an early age because her mother remained sick. Shakuntala did not remember her mother ever being well and able. Hence there was no question of Shakuntala going to school.

Younger siblings had arrived one after the other. In Shakuntala's words, "Inspite of her illness, Mother was able to produce a child every year and it used to make me very angry. I used to ask her, 'What will you do with so many children?'" It added to her work, as child care was more or less complctely left to Shakuntala. Three children born after her were boys and hence were no help to her in housework.

Shakuntala deeply regretted not having had the opportunity to go to school. She placed high value on education, more so for girls as, "Girls have to bring up their children and maintain the home". About her own future she said, "Whether I can feed my children properly or not, I'll definitely give them an education."

At the time of interview, Shakuntala was attending adult education classes at the Jesus and Mary College and was finding it a very rewarding experience. She was so taken up with this new experience that she studied for hours together at home. She had instructed her family that once she sat down with her books, she should not be disturbed or asked to do housework. She said, "I've told them, I've done my share of work at the time when I should have been studying, so don't stop me from studying now".

Shakuntala had not only brought up the younger siblings, she had also become a person with power and authority in the family. She had the keys of the house, no decisions were made without consulting her. In a society where girls are generally dominated by their brothers, Shakuntala had a fair amount of control over her brothers. She did not give them much housework to do because "They had to study", but expected them to be home before time to sleep. She had threatened them that if they came too late, say after a late night film, she would not open the door for them, serve dinner or let them have a bed.

To add to the family income Shakuntala was running a small part time vegetable shop near her house with the help of her brothers. It yielded about Rs.150/- per month. She preferred it to a sweeper's job which was the caste occupation. Apart from this, whenever she found time, Shakuntala stitched clothes for others and made a few rupees. She aspired to find a 'respectable' job in a factory or an office eventually.

Shakuntala had not felt that there was any discrimination made between her and her brothers. This was probably because she herself was an important figure in the family. She was allowed to go out, spend money and even see a movie once in a while. She felt that girls should be treated as equals with boys in all aspects, including education.

Like many other girls of her social class, Shakuntala wished to be a boy in her "next birth". Her main reason was that she wanted to be educated. Another reason was personal autonomy, which she phrased thus, "Girls have to go away to their in laws' house after marriage where they have to serve them and do as they are told".

Shakuntala entered menarche totally unaware of this stage of life. The day she started her first menstrual period, she did not notice anything until a friend pointed out to her that she had stained her *salwar*. She was gripped by fear and started crying thinking she had done something wrong. Her friend gave her advice on how she should equip herself in the situation. Later Shakuntala told her mother who did not volunteer any comment. For many years afterwards Shakuntala did not accept menstrual periods as a part of life and resented them. She felt that her mother should have talked to her about it before the onset of menarche.

Marriage did not appeal to Shakuntala as a goal in life. She thought that if one could make her own living, there was no need to get married. But at the same time she knew that this view would not be acceptable to her parents, who were already in search of a match for her. She also knew that her opinion would not be sought though she wished to be consulted. She would have to marry whoever was selected by her parents.

Shakuntala's case has been presented not because she represents a typical lower class adolescent girl, but because the circumstances in which she grew up were quite typical of the lower social class. She was unusual because she had taken up adult roles and responsibilities from a very early age and wielded power within the family, not common to girls in her social group. The value she had for formal education was symbolic of the need to free herself from the routines of child rearing and domesticity.

Shakuntala had a sense of personal and social identity. She did not reject femininity, but repudiated the limitations attached to the female role, recognising the privileges of being a boy.

In sum, Shakuntala did not give the impression of being an adolescent working out her sense of identity, but of a mature young woman, who had weathered many crises and had built up certain convictions that were guiding her life.

Urban Middle SES

There was a wide range of responses among the subjects of the middle SES urban group. The girls varied widely in their perceptions on the variables of aspiration level, perception of sex discrimination in socialisation, satisfaction with sex role and circumstances and control in marriage. Quite often, half the number of girls indicated a view quite contrary to what the other half had expressed.

In this group of adolescent girls, not only were the subjects widely distributed in their perspectives, they were also exposed to the contradictory demands of their parents. The parents desired a harmonious amalgam of high achievement and high conformity to sex typed behaviour in their daughters.

One significant pointer towards the value for achievement was that education for girls was considered obligatory and not a matter of choice, both by the girls and their parents. The question was how much, rather than whether or not. Completing graduation seemed to be the mode, coupled with aspirations to take up careers fairly seriously. The parents expected their daughters to devote a good part of their day towards academic work and to compete well with their peers in tests and examinations. Anju's father, a clerk with Delhi Transport Corporation, had high expectations from her, the eldest of three daughters. He had told her, "Study as much as your aptitude permits so that you can earn respect in the society.... I want to see you with a good designation."

The fact that every single girl in the group wanted to have a job and did not, in general, see her parents objecting to this, indicated that the middle class parent saw his or her daughter also in an occupational role. The girl was expected to be achievement oriented and suitably equipped with the potential to earn. This was seen to increase her eligibility for marriage and to serve as a safeguard against misfortunes such as the death of the husband or separation from him due to disharmony or divorce. It would not be presumptuous to believe that the media coverage of harassment of women on economic grounds, and separation of married couples in urban areas, had its impact on these girls. The potential to be economically independent was an imperative, in this context.

The girls perceived their educational qualification as a strength that would help them become an economic asset to their families. The ability to be able to earn was seen as an insurance against the personal tragedy of widowhood or separation. It can be deduced that they would rather be separated than be harassed.

Working outside the home was valued highly among the girls. A working girl's status was perceived to be higher than that of a housewife. Working primarily to achieve economic independence in matters of personal expenditure was the motive of nearly half the number of girls. This signified their underlying need to achieve some degree of autonomy. Being able to contribute towards family income would also give them a greater role in deciding their own future. Neelam, who was the youngest of 10 children of a small scale businessman felt that, "If a girl is working, she is not a burden on anyone; her prestige goes up, and her in-laws also get along with her as she spends only a part of the day in the house. The main reason why I want to work is that I want to do what I like and not what my parents want me to do.... If a girl is capable of earning, it is good, she does not have to plead for money even if it is her parents she has to ask.... I have seen that girls who earn do not have restrictions on them, whether they accumulate a bank balance or spend the money".

The number of girls how reported discrimination between boys and girls in socialisation at home was the same as in the lower SES group. However, the implications of this similarity are different in this class. In a set-up where daughters are given higher education and expected to take a job, marked sex differences in socialisation are not conducive for a positive sense of identity. Manju, who wanted to become a lawyer, wished that she had been a boy because, "As a girl one has to produce children, bring them up and look after the husband. As a boy, you don't have to do any of these things."

Another subject, Neelam wished to be born a boy in the 'next birth' because she could not, at the moment, fulfil her wish to see movies. She said, "Even if today somebody can transform me into a boy, I'd be willing..... and I'd keep sitting in a theatre all day long". It can be seen that while education *per se* was emphasized by the parents, its natural concomitants such as freedom of thought and action were not recognized by them. In fact, a review of the qualities emphasized by the parents for their daughters showed that the girls were expected to cultivate docility and conformity in conduct. Thus, by emphasizing somewhat contradictory goals, the socialisers were posing dilemma for the girls.

The major grudge of the girls, as in the lower SES sample, was the relatively greater freedom of movement to boys. Anita was the youngest of 10 children, most of whom were married. She was dominated by her brothers which she greatly resented. Her attempts to go out to meet her friends were thwarted by them as they did not let her go alone. She said, "It irritates me a lot that I am not allowed by them to go out when they can go anywhere they like."

The middle SES girls were quite articulate in expressing their disapproval of the discriminatory practices. Yet, a large number felt that these differences were inevitable as they corresponded to the norms of society. The dissonance between what the girls desired as individuals and what they accepted as social sanction was a factor contributing towards ambivalence and a rejection of their gender. The wish to be male rather than female (in the next birth) was widely expressed. An antecedent of general dissatisfaction among these girls was their lack of autonomy.

In contrast to this, a number of girls (16) were quite happy with being female, most of whom wished to be born female again (in their next birth). These girls did not necessarily have more freedom than others but were comfortable in their roles and felt that they were not at a disadvantage compared to boys. Neena, who had a younger brother and was doing Medicine, remarked, "Girls are more sensitive while boys are quite selfish and impulsive .... I think, at any age, girls are always more mature than boys." The envy of the male was pervasive due to his freedom but as a rule there was an acceptance of the rules.

The pattern of bi-modal distribution of subjects was evident in many ways. There were those who felt autonomous despite the limitations while there were some who felt extremely restricted. There were girls who had a sense of direction and were guided by their convictions towards their life goals, while others conveyed an absence of directionality and a lack of commitment to any principles or ideals. On another level, there were girls who gave the impression that they anticipated an active role in determining their future pattern of life. As against this, many girls felt helpless in the face of their circumstances.

The expression of discontent among the girls in this group does not imply that they actually had no freedom. The results indicated that there was more freedom allowed to these girls than to the lower SES girls, but it was not perceived as sufficient. The burden of housework was not heavy; however, they considered some housework as part of their daily routine, whether studying or working. It was generally felt by the girls that boys should also be expected to help in housework. They attributed their brothers' lack of contribution to housework to lower parental control of boys.

In several ways, the middle SES girls had opportunities for social interaction outside their home. Since they were attending either a school or a college, all of them had friends. However, checks on their friendships and restrictions on the time spent with peers were maintained by parents and brothers.

Physical changes preceding and following menarche were not seen as having taken place abruptly by the girls. The only physical event that they could recall was their first menstrual period. This experience had been unpleasant for most girls mainly because of the fact that they had no knowledge about it beforehand. Shobha, whose parents were educated, was 13 years old when she had her menarche. She had no prior knowledge about it. In her words, "I was doing my Sanskrit paper. I got up to borrow something from the girl in front of me. The girl sitting behind me must have noticed that I had messed up my dress. She took me to the teacher. I had not completed my paper. The teacher said, 'You can go home, I will give you marks on the basis of your previous marks.' She did not tell me anything else. She sent me home along with another girl..... Mummy asked me, 'What happened'? and I told her everything... She told me that this happens with every girl. I cried a lot, I was feeling very odd, as if I had committed a crime. That day I did not have my food. For two or three days, I felt awful".

Girls in this group could identify the subtle maturational changes in themselves, both psychological and physical. Some of them could verbalise their feelings of awkwardness and heightened awareness of new sensations. Their perceptions of themselves as individuals filtered through their responses. This increased sensitivity of the self and its expression can be partly attributed to their higher levels of education and a somewhat free environment.

The mother was a distant person, and not a friend. Not one mother had prepared her daughter for menarche, though a number of girls felt that she was the right person to have taken this responsibility. Although the mother was mentioned more often than the father as the person who monitored the girl's behaviour, she did not emerge as a model who the daughter admired. The father was seen as an approachable figure who invariably had an active role in determining the girl's level and type of education. In fact, discrimination between boys and girls in the house was reportedly shown more by the mother than by the father.

The middle class adolescent girl did not perceive her marriage as imminent. She saw it as an event that would take place after a couple of years, when she had completed her education and perhaps worked for a while. The fact that a few even contemplated not getting married at all could be an indication of their pre-occupation with other issues at that time, or it could be a defensive reaction to their total pre-occupation with the idea of marriage. Ranjana, who was, in general, fairly conventional in her responses and did not perceive many sex differences in socialisation in her own home, said, "I haven't yet thought about marriage at all.... I do not want to get married, I have no interest (in marriage). I want to be a teacher and teach."

There were many other indicators of greater autonomy and individuality among middle class girls compared to their lower class counterparts. The subjects perceived and probably had greater control over matters related to their own marriage. Selecting their partner in marriage was not an impossible idea for many girls. In fact, half of them did not view marriage as essential for life. Yet, the traditional pattern of the daughter-in-law living in the joint family rather than living independently with her husband, was preferred. The girls said that they expected the daughter-in-law to adapt herself to the way of her husband's family.

What seemed to emerge as a pattern of the middle class girl was that her urge to seek an ego identity was frustrated by her need to conform to a socially approved identity, which demanded devaluation of individuality as a principle. While her wish to achieve and the need to exercise autonomy signified the need to work out a sense of self identity, parental injunctions, taboos and fear of social stigma shaped her behaviour towards group conformity. The need for social approval was as distinct as was the need to be recognized as an individual.

It was apparent that there was a distance between the gender role and the identity of the self as an individual. It is as if every girl dissociated herself from the rest of the population of typical females who had a prescribed social role. So when she expressed resentment of the female status and role, she somehow excluded herself from the victimised group and appeared to hold herself in high esteem. She invariably conformed to the culturally prescribed role, and at the same time aspired for liberties that were associated with the status of the opposite sex. There cannot be a simple analysis of why such conflicting feelings emerged. It might be suggested that the socio-psychological environment of the girls engendered values that fostered individuality. At the same time, there was negative reinforcement for egocentric behaviour. In the face of such a predicament the girls experienced inner conflicts and, in some cases, a crisis of identity.

Case Profile

Pushpa Kumari

The case of Pushpa was selected for detailed analysis because she was one subject whose crisis of identity was quite apparent due to the conflicts between what she desired and what was actually happening.

Pushpa, 19, was the eldest of seven children of a clerk. The family lived in the village Humayunpur in New Delhi. There were four rooms in the house, two of which were rented out. Just prior to the interview Pushpa had appeared for her B.A. final year examination.

Pushpa's marriage was fixed when she had completed her schooling. However, she had wanted to study further and her father was also in favour of her completing graduation and the marriage was postponed until the end of her education. Now that her examination was over, Pushpa was to be married in a few days' time.

Both these issues, that is, her final year examination as well as her impending marriage, were points of anxiety for Pushpa. From the moment the interview started Pushpa broke into a monologue on how unhappy she was about her performance in the examination and feared that she might fail. According to her she had been suffering from an illness for a long time and had, therefore, not been able to study to her satisfaction. There were tears in her eyes when she said, "I used to consider myself quite competent. But I could not do as well (academically) as I wanted to .... I feel as though all this is happening with somebody else and not with me".

Pushpa's anxiety about failure in her examination was aggravated by her forthcoming marriage. She was afraid that once married she would not able to reappear for the examination in case she failed. Thus she would lose her B.A. degree, something she valued a great deal. In fact her anxiety on this account was so high that she was not looking forward to the marriage at all. She seemed almost certain that the marriage would bring an end to all her ambitions. She had wanted to work outside the home and earn for sometime before getting married. Pushpa believed that she was being married off too soon after her education. She said, "If I was not getting married, I would have had a job - such as an office job or I would have taken a training course".

Pushpa's uncertainty about herself was revealed when she could not say in any definite terms as to what type of career she wanted. She could only indicate that she wanted to work to be economically self sufficient. Her need to be economically productive was persistent, but what means she would adopt was not clear. In her words, I won't sit at home. If I fail in B.A. I will repeat the examination."

Although Pushpa had got engaged three years earlier, she had not been able to reconcile to the fact that she would not have the opportunity to work and learn further before marriage. She believed in equal opportunity for women and valued education as a fundamental right. It appeared that Pushpa equated her failure in the B.A. examination to the loss of an identity that she had been building for herself. Her belief that women should also work seemed to her to be in conflict with her role after marriage. She said that it was more important to achieve something rather than to simply get married.

In Pushpa's case the crisis was at a personal level, affecting her ego identity. She was performing her social role without any sign of breakdown. Doing housework was part of Pushpa's daily routine before and after college time. She did this willingly and did not crave for more independence than she already had. She said that she was quite happy in the female role and would like to be born a girl even in the 'next birth'. As a girl also one can improve upon one's life... We can achieve the same things as girls that boys do."

Pushpa entered menarche at the age of 14. She had some idea about it through her friends, and hence could cope with the situation herself. She did not inform her mother when she entered menarche because "I cannot talk frankly with my mother". It was a cousin with whom Pushpa discussed it.

In mental health terms Pushpa's crisis of identity had a positive aspect to it. Her introspection had led to a state of dilemma in the face of visible options. Realising her potentialities she resisted acquiescing to a lack of control. Her feeling of worthlessness had an undercurrent of faith in her ability to be an individual.

Urban Upper SES

The upper SES urban girl emerged as a person with ego-strength and a strong sense of identity. Although she was confronted with various conflicts at different stages during her adolescence, she had fewer contradictions in her life than her middle SES counterpart. In more than one way, the upper SES girls stood out from the other two urban groups.

The values of the girl in this group relating to education, career and marriage were different from those of the middle SES girls. They did not value a high level of formal education *per se*. Acquiring college degrees was not the only concept of education among them. From the point of view of employment, doing a vocational course after school was considered more useful than a bachelor's degree.

Having a career in the future was seen as an important development objective. A job was valued not only because it helped to discontinue dependence on parents for personal expenses and to improve one's status, but also for others reasons. According to Mala, "Once a girl starts working it strengthens her .... She develops individuality, she thinks originally.... I want to work, to stand on my own feet. I will be able to have a broader perspective of life and meet different people."

Giving another point of view, Malini said, "My main aim in wanting to work is to get satisfaction that I've achieved something in life. I've spent so many years on my education.... I don't want to be a burden on my family..... I know my parents will be proud of me if I take up a lecturership." Adopting a more practical approach Seema elaborated, "Why I want to work is a combination of many things. I want to be independent, also to do something extra outside the house, to increase money in the family, to take advantage of my education and to meet people."

The upper SES girls were not under pressure to work. Their parents did not put undue emphasis on academic achievement as is indicated by the finding that only five girls reported parental concern with their achievement in school or college. The girls had adopted the attitude that they would study only as much as they themselves thought necessary and would work if their parents and circumstances permitted. Since university degrees were not essential to pursue a vocational course, having college education was not deemed necessary. Mamta, who was a school-going girl maintained, "It is not necessary that girls must have very high education. If my parents are satisfied, I want to stop after 12th and join some course; I don't want to join college."

Indecisiveness regarding the future goal (mostly academic) was a common trait of the school going girls, though not totally absent among the college girls. In view of the fact that adolescents do have several options after they have completed their school/college education, the girls generally did not have a specific goal in their mind. Quite often there were many choices and the girl would have had to redefine her interests and re-evaluate her own potential before finally deciding.

The exercise of choosing among several options did not seem to be a serious problem. The girls knew that several factors would determine the final decision, and that their own interest was a secondary determinant. Their results in the last examination, their eligibility for the course desired, their performance on the qualifying test for that course and their parents' preference were some of the main factors that determined their selection of a given option. The problem was deeper for a girl who was eligible for several options but was compelled by her parents to adopt the one she did not desire. She then entered the new field with the assumption that she would not like it. Such an experience produced interference in the crystalisation of her vocational aspirations. There were four girls who had been persuaded to join courses despite their unwillingness.

The other girls were realistic as well as optimistic about their future. They had worked out alternative options to guard themselves against the situation of being left without a job. Mala recounted her earlier interest in Medicine and a change of mind subsequently. "From the very beginning when I was young I wanted to be a doctor. Now when I am doing Medical subjects (in school) I don't think I want to be a doctor. It was just infatuation.... I think its' not a line for me. Its' very tough. There's a lot of competition. It don't want to slog. The doctors are supposed to slog all their lives". Talking about her present interests she said, "I want to do a language so that I can work in an embassy or as ground duty hostess with some airlines. I can work as an interpreter..... My older sister tells me to do Psychology Honours. Another friend of mine who is doing Psychology Honours is also encouraging me to do Psychology."

A first year student of B.A, Ruchi provided a good example of an adolescent who wanted a career but was not sure in which field. Although unsure she was quite optimistic, perhaps unduly so. "I want to sit for I.A.S. and all the competitive examinations. If I don't get into I.A.S., I want to do journalism or something like that. But I haven't decided yet. I might do M.A. I am interested in a lecturer's job also. I plan to do Ph.D. also. There are bank exams. After doing graduation one can do Law or B.Ed."

A glance at the responses of the upper SES girls revealed that they had fairly good opportunities for higher education and for following a career. They had freedom to form peer group affiliations, and to determine their personal matters. They could choose not to do housework. They anticipated sufficient self control over their marriages and enjoyed a comfortable rapport with their parents. In short, they had more freedom than their lower and middle SES counterparts. However, half the number of girls in the group perceived a gender discrimination in parental attitudes and behaviour. They felt that more restrictions were exercised on them than on their brothers. When the restriction was related to travelling alone or coming home after dark, the girls were willing to concede that such constraints were necessary to ensure physical safety. But if there was interference in their relations with friends, or in selecting academic subjects or in marriage plans, the girls resented it and conveyed their feelings directly to their parents.

The fact that they could differ from their parents is an indication of a certain level of freedom and of parity with boys. Hence it is significant that even the slightest preference for boys shown by parents (the mother being most commonly the parent responsible) was noticed and resented by the girls. Samina who had two sisters and a brother commented that her mother cared specially for her brother. She observed, "When he comes from college Mummy always gets up and brings food for him. When we come, even though we are tired, she says, 'O.K. go and take it' or 'Shall I get up?' Then we say, 'Of course not'. We don't mind but we feel it, 'Why not for us?' Even we are tired and we look forward to Mummy getting up and saying 'Have this or have that'."

One outstanding feature of the upper SES girls as a group was that they showed evidence of introspection. They seemed to be engaged in thinking about themselves. Almost every girl appeared to be evaluating her own status, talking about her own specific needs and traits as well as judging her relationship with others. Discussing the change in herself with age, Seema said, "First I never used to take notice of me. Now I have become more conscious of how people think of me, how I look. I started questioning myself like - I should have a certain aim in life and I should have some hobbies and I should develop certain interests." Another subject's self appraisal was, "Over the years I think I've become obstinate. I want to do whatever I feel like. May be I don't feel like doing (What I'm told) because my parents keep saying "you have become obstinate'."

Introspection on philosophical issues, not always personal, was also found to take place. Pained by general apathy among people towards others Kavita reported that she used to "Just keep thinking of why people are so complicated and why so many times unwittingly they cause so much of hurt..... It had a greater meaning (for me) to achieve happiness as a person, to bring happiness to others not me individually, (but) as a (member of the) human race."

Being in contradictory states of mind is one of the adolescent traits. When asked to comment on whether or not she was satisfied with her circumstances Puja said, "I am fairly satisfied but I am such a restless person that I get dissatisfied very soon. I am very temperamental. I am very optimistic, yet very pessimistic. If two days things don't turn out to be the way I want I'd say, I'm going to commit suicide.' Its' my favourite fib".

It is significant to note that while a number of girls (20) expressed satisfaction with their present sex identity, only 13 out of these wished to be born female in their 'next birth'. A related finding was that 21 girls were dissatisfied with their existing circumstances. A deeper probe into the responses of the subjects revealed the implications of these figures. It was noted that the subjects had not once attributed any action to Fate or God. They were specific in mentioning their choices and hypotheses. It may be recalled that this group was the least traditional on the Traditionality Scale.

There were other indications, as shown by the results, to confirm the fact that these girls believed in-and actually had - substantial control over their own life circumstances, events and future plans. Hence an attitude of dissatisfaction towards a particular situation, such as parents' disapproving inter caste marriage, implied that the girl would try to bring about a change in her parents. She had an awareness of alternative ways of living and thinking. These are indications of individual attempts to resist conformity to unfounded beliefs, to challenge the socialising agents and to initiate a rebellion against the philosophy of discrimination.

The discrepancy between the figures of the option for the male sex in the 'next birth' and the figures related to satisfaction with the female role at present can also be explained. The upper SES girls probably viewed the concept of another birth as a purely hypothetical situation and not as something that they could trust to be true. Hence they responded to the question about 'next birth' as if what they wished was only imaginary, a vicarious wish fulfilment. Thus some of those who expressed satisfaction with their present sex identity gave preference for being born male. However, the fact that the girls identified with their present gender with all the limitations of femaleness was evidence of their acceptance of their identity.

One point that needs to be raised here to understand the respondents' behaviour is that in any research which has to depend completely on their reported information, the possibility of spurious responses and those given without much thought, cannot be ruled out. Hence figures *per se* cannot be used to derive the full meaning, although they are meaningful. The impressions obtained through the interview are equally important and need careful consideration when interpreting the figures into results.

The upper SES girls had their own share of conflicts. These were not always related to everyday interactions within the family or elsewhere. There was instances of very specific individualised crises. One subject hopelessly wishes to go back to the age of 14-15 years. She said, "There are too many hassles when you grow up.... I generally feel disgusted in a way. I think childhood is so free. Do anything, there are no worries. Even if you do something wrong, you are considered to be innocent. I want to remain 14-15 years, neither younger nor older".

Facing a different kind of crisis Bela wished to marry a boy who did not belong to her own caste. But she was in a conflict. She said, "In our family they don't allow inter caste marriages... If I want to have an inter caste marriage my mother will seriously object to it. The person I have liked is not from my caste... Though I haven't made up my mind about this, I won't be able to go against wishes of my parents."

Talking about crises, Kiran was a text book case of an adolescent going through identity confusion. She admitted to not having any ambition in particular. Narrating how and when this change towards a non-goal took place she said, "I was about 14-15 years then. I just stopped thinking of vocational ambitions, say becoming a doctor, or an engineer. I just sopped thinking of these things.... I'm still going through a very funny kind of phase which sometimes really upsets me. I became very confused as a person and I still am. I lost that old confidence. I didn't see (that) it was very important to know what I wanted to be as a person really, as (it was) to be happy for the present which I am not." Having gone through emotional upheaval herself due to discord between her parents, her one inner need was to be able to bring happiness to others, but she did not know how to do it." To me it's very important that people should be happy... The very concept of giving happiness gives me a lot of happiness. But I cannot pinpoint in particular that I want to be a lawyer or anything.... In fact I find it hard to be specific about anything." However, Kavita was not a typical case. Most girls were able to indicate the direction of their goals and ambitions, if not definitely, at least tentatively.

The girls in the upper SES were not the most articulate about their experiences of change during puberty and the emotions accompanying them. While growth spurts at adolescence were perceived as natural, most girls felt that their growth had been gradual. A few excepts from their interviews would confirm this finding.

- I didn't feel any great physical change. Mentally, I think, I felt I was growing. I felt I grew more or faster than my friends in 10th and 11th (std.) mentally. Though of course I used to behave like them, at time I felt that they behaved like juveniles (Renu).
- I myself never felt that I've grown up suddenly or any such thing. I still think of myself as a kid. The way I talk people still find me very kiddish. Of course, I've matured quite a bit from the point of view of relationship with other people (Ruchi).
- I grew gradually, I become conscious of the change. You become much more shy, you don't go out all that often. At this age, initially you do feel that you are a female. Emotions also change. I have become sensitive. My parents tell me that I've become much more irritable (Neena).

There were three girls whose realisations at puberty of the fact that they were unlike boys was traumatic. Two girls were the third daughters in their family and said that they had been quite boy-like in their dress and behaviour pattern. Anita's experience of growing up changed her substantially. She said, "My mother always wanted a son, so I always liked to act like a tomboy. I was brought up in that sort of atmosphere that I wanted to play marbles rather than play with dolls.... I had quite a few friends who were male.... Once I started my periods I became entirely different. My attitude towards them also changed.... I became a little bit awkward with them and when they asked me 'What's wrong'? I felt quite awkward and shy to tell them anything."

Purnima also used to dress up like a boy until she joined college. Once in college, she felt the need to change and to act like a girl. She admitted "I resented the change because I would have definitely liked to continue to be a tomboy....I became conscious of boys in college and that is one of the reasons why I had to change myself and I resented this fact."

The third subject Puja narrated her experience of the realisation of the difference between the two sexes in very dramatic terms. According to her, when she was in a convent school during her early school years, the nuns had told the girls that boys were girls with their hair cut. Puja said that she had believed it until one day at 13 years of age she noticed that boys had a moustache. In her words, "I could not believe it, it was so strange.... The change struck me.... It was horrible. I'd never like to go through it again. I was so confused... One fine morning it struck me that may be we are not the same. I started reading lots of books and talking to my friends."

The feeling of neither being a child nor an adult during early adolescent, was reported by many girls. Kamal related the experience of being chided by her mother for 'immature' behaviour on various occasions saying, "You're not a kid anymore". But if she sat among older people she was told, "You are not yet grown up enough". Recounting her exasperation Kamal said, "You are not among the children and you've not among the grown ups. You don't know where to go unless you have people your own age group." Renu admitted feeling uncertain in the past. She said, "I did go through a period when you don't know whether you belong to the kids or to the adults."

Textbook like descriptions of perception of changes in themselves were provided by the upper SES girls. There were subjects whose experience of feeling "on stage" was very vivid. Rina, 16 years old, was uneasy when out with her family. She said, "When we go out, I keep my mouth shut. I don't even get up (to go) from one place to another, otherwise I feel that everybody is watching me. If a button (on my dress) is missing, then also I feel that everybody is watching that this girl's button is missing. I don't know why I have this consciousness, I don't even eat there, I can not eat. Mummy tells me, 'Eat Rina, everybody is eating their own food and not watching you'. But I say, 'No, I won't eat'."

Rekha had shot up by 7" in height in 1 1/2 years after 15 years of age. She was confused as to how exactly she had felt then. She could recall, "There was a stage when I was very embarrassed about everything, I felt, everything I said or did.... everybody was looking at me.... I wouldn't stand up in class and talk because I thought everybody would say that 'She's spoken'. But it kind of passed."

One subject, who conveyed the feeling that she was enjoying growing up said, "Mentally I (have) changed. I feel grown up. Thoughts were different. Interests changed. I want to be independent, do whatever I like, think about things. Boys notice me more, try to talk with me. I've also become conscious of them. Like everybody I also like to look nice. You feel like dressing up the best when you go out" (Mamta). While talking about her marriage Mamta quipped amusingly, "I don't know what will happen. I think I'll fall in love even before they (parents) find somebody. That's why I don't want to go to college. If I meet a Punjabi (fellow) my parents won't approve. So I am scared. Everybody falls in love at this stage."

Preference for solitude was expressed by many adolescents either as a need at present or in the past. "There was this stage when I never liked going out with my parents or anybody. I wanted to be with myself alone. The very thought of going out in a group .... I would dread.... I just used to be day-dreaming and hated going out said Kavita.

Parental expectations regarding their daughters' behaviour were quite stereotypical. In the girls' perception the parents emphasised the characteristics of being homely, subdued and 'feminine' as against 'tomboyish'. According to Mala, "I think they don't want me to be as chirpy as I am. They don't want me to be tomboyish. Both Bela (her twin sister) and I are a bit tomboyish. About other things they want me to know everything; such as household work; that I should know how to behave with boys and I should respect my elders. I should be able to speak sweetly with everybody and not keep fighting in the house." Another 19-year-old said, "They want me to be soft spoken, (be) aware of all the things, (be) good in everything and academically also good. In short I should be a 'good girl'." The goal for which these traits were desirable was a 'good' marriage. Parents made frequent mention of 'what will others say?' to make the girls conform to socially desirable behaviour. The imaginary future mother-in-law was brought in to urge the girls to learn household skills.

However, flexibility rather than rigidity or authoritarianism seemed to be the pattern in parental disciplining. There were indications of a rapport between the girls and at least one parent, if not both. Some girls mentioned being closer to the mother while some others were more fond of the father. "I'm most attached to my father. I'm his favourite though he doesn't have much time" was Rina's remark. Riti also spoke of her father as someone who understood her more than her mother did, "He can really predict what I'm going to say next. He can also make my mother understand me. My mother doesn't sometimes understand things, so he explains to her."

Kavita was very close to her mother and appreciated her sensitivity, "My mother is very understanding ... Till I was in P.U.C.* my mother had great expectations because I was meant to be very brilliant in my talking, carrying myself and so on. She expected a lot ... At that time I was very interested in sitting for the I.F.S.** But after that she herself started seeing the change in me. She's never said she wants me to become something after that. She's accepted that fact that I'll do what I want to for the time being. And she's accepted the fact that I'm not very particular about what I want to do.... My mother reacted according to my state of mind. She didn't force it on me. She wanted me to be happy."

While discussing her ambitions Samina became very pensive

---

* One year pre-university course.

** Indian Foreign Services.

and said, "What I really wanted and I know it won't be true is to live with my parents. I want that my sisters and brother should get married while I stay with my parents, work and come back home to them.....Although a boy should feel like that I don't know why I don't want to be parted from them. I'm very attached to them, specially to my father. I feel its too much to go on your own and live your own life and leave your parents behind." Realizing the futility of her wish she added, "May be I'm too young and that's why I think like that. May be five years later I'll think differently." Samina had a brother who, she thought, would not really care for their parents once he had his own family.

Parents' trust in them was valued by the daughters and was also the basis of attachment or resentment in the relationship. Kirti said confidently, "I know my parents have so much faith in me that when I want to do something wrong I can't do it. When I do something I feel my mother knows that I've done it." Renu supported her parents for imposing more limitations on her movements as compared to her brothers. She explained, "I've never felt restricted. If there were restrictions I think they were justified-parents have to be more careful with regard to girls.... In fact some of the girls used to say, I wish we had parents like yours. Probably I am very lucky that they are so understanding and they understood me. I know what they would like me to do".

The mother was a friend to many girls, who could talk about their experiences and problems with her. "She is more like a friend to me" said Ruchi, "I discuss everything with her. Because I take her into confidence concerning every aspect and I discuss with her everything. She knows she can rely on me. She really trusts me. I also don't let her down".

To sum up, the upper SES girl was going through the 'bridge period' with a certain amount of independence that was only sporadically found among middle SES girls and almost missing among the lower SES girls. She had the time and the opportunity to make important decisions regarding her education and career that sometimes engulfed her in a dilemma. The impact of the crisis was softened as she could choose the less difficult alternative of not wanting to achieve very much. Apathy towards achievement or inability to establish an occupational identity did not lead to a lowered self concept. Economic independence and an occupational role were not the necessary concomitants of a woman's identity.

If the girl selected the more difficult alternative of working towards achievement and a career, she had parental support until she got married. It was significant that despite situations where choices lead to conflict and non-resolution of conflicts lead to crises, the adolescent girl maintained a sense of identity. The process of crystallisation of identity was not yet complete; however, there was no confusion of identity. Most of them occupied the status of adolescents where adult responsibilities were not thrust upon them, and the subjects felt that they had left their childhood behind. They had the opportunity to experiment with several roles before deciding which role they would eventually assume.

Case Profile

Madhu Kalra

"If society is still like what it is then I would definitely like to be a boy in the 'next birth'. These were the words in which Madhu reflected her frustration of being female. A cynical but a lively girl, Madhu, 17 yrs. 6 months, was a short, petite and attractive young woman. When she was interviewed she had just completed her 12th std. examination from a public school in Delhi. Madhu's father was in an executive post in a prominent public sector company, while her mother was a school teacher. Madhu had a 13 years old brother. The family lived in an upper middle class neighbourhood.

Madhu was selected for the case profile for several reasons. She was quite articulate about her experience and feelings. She reflected several attitudes that could be representative of the attitudes of most upper SES girls studied. She was also exceptional in that she was quite clear about her principles in life and was critical of following a beaten path. In a way she also represented a majority who thought like her but who were not able to verablise their thoughts coherently and strongly enough.

Madhu struck the interviewer as an ambitious, assertive and independent girl. She believed in equal rights for men and women and maintained that higher education was as important for girls as it was for boys. According to her, going out to work was in no way only a man's privilege or responsibility. She hoped to marry someone who would let her work.

Madhu wanted to become a chartered accountant and had therefore taken up Commerce as the main subject in school. She wanted to follow up the same line of education in college. Her parents had not interfered in her selection of this field of study and had told her that she could study as much as she wanted to.

Why did she want to work? "Because I just want to work" was Madhu's reply. She further elaborated, "Naturally, you become financially independent. You have some meaning in your life. You have studied for so many years, it occupies your time instead of just sitting and gossipping." Madhu did not want to be financially dependent on anyone even after her marriage.

Unlike most of the subjects in this group the relations between Madhu and her mother appeared to be strained. The cause, as mentioned by Madhu, was her lack of interest in housework and in learning skills like cooking and stitching. In her words, "I have to do it (housework) because I am a girl. If I were a boy then I wouldn't have done it. I am generally not fond of housework so I don't like doing it, and that too when there's a difference between a girl and a boy." Her mother's constant reminder to Madhu was "Whether you become a doctor or a lawyer, you will land up in the kitchen." Madhu was infuriated by her mother's often repeated remark, "What will your mother-in-law say?" She expressed indignation at this attitude of doing things for the sake of social approval in the future. She admitted to rebelling against doing anything that she was expected to do for the sake of conformity. This often lead to arguments between her and her mother.

Another issue on which Madhu expressed strong views was her parents' attitude of discrimination between herself and her brother. She felt that he was more free than she was to do what he wanted. He could go out to play for hours without being told to attend to any work related to the house while she was expected to do housework regularly. Madhu believed that "everything should be shared between a girl and her brother. If one person is given certain privileges, the other person should also be able to share them, or get something in return. It should not be one sided."

Madhu's parents, specially her mother, did not seem to trust her fully. They kept an obvious check on her in many ways. For example, when she made a new friend, she was asked a lot of questions about her and her family in a way which made Madhu feel uncomfortable. For the same reason Madhu tried not to visit her friends who lived far, because then she was confronted with a volley of questions about her visit. Inspite of being in a co-educational school, Madhu did not interact with her male classmates outside the school because her mother disapproved of her doing so.

When Madhu came of age at 13, she entered menarche with an extremely negative attitude towards menstruation. According to her, she had a faint idea about it before it occurred, but she did not expect it "so soon". When she was told that the menstrual cycle was part of life for a woman, she was disgusted, "I just hated it. I wanted to finish off with life at that very moment, I felt so terrible!..... That was the first time when I felt that I should have been a boy."

Psychologically Madhu had experienced and was still going through 'adolescent' experiences. There was a time when she used to feel 'on stage'. She had felt that everyone around her was looking only at her, and that she could not look people in their face. However, Madhu reported that she had got over that stage. She said that she often indulged in day dreaming, "Sometimes when I'm studying I start day dreaming. It may be a simple word like 'but' that starts if off." Madhu preferred solitude at home. She wished that no one would ask her anything about what she was doing or planning to do with her time.

Madhu's determination to be individualistic came through in her views about her marriage as well. She seemed quite sure that she would select her life partner herself and would not be willing to accept an arranged marriage. Although she did not perceive her marriage as imminent, she was confident that she would exercise a substantial amount of control over the situation when the time came. While talking about it she mentioned that she would not like to live in a joint family after marriage as "there are too many religious rites and rituals (to be observed when living with the older generation) which I find meaningless."

It was quite apparent that Madhu expected something quite different out of her life than what she was getting. When asked whether she was satisfied with her circumstances her response was, "I wish that I was born in a different sort of family - more liberal." Her resentment towards her family was understandable in view of the fact that her parents wanted her to be homely, obedient and 'Indian', may be as against Western." An Indian girl for them probably was one who had incorporated the first two traits. Not surprisingly Madhu said that she did not like being an Indian. Perhaps she was consciously making an effort to not to come close to her parents' model of being an 'Indian' girl. Quite exasperated with the conservative attitudes of the society in general she wished that "People around her would change their attitudes with changing times."

In an overall analysis it is evident that Madhu's case is that of an adolescent who grows up in a family that permits a fair amount of freedom to its daughters when they are children. The girls go to English medium schools, acquire Western values and aim at a high level of education and career. However, as they approach adolescence, the parents suddenly realise that their daughter has become independent and does not approximate the model of a 'nice' girl.

Social approval of the daughter is more important to the parents than that of their son. So they being to coax the girl to take interest in the socially prescribed female task of housekeeping. They impose curbs on her behaviour in the hope that they can prevent her from acting autonomously. They try to fit her into the socially acceptable roles of a skilled housekeeper and a well behaved daughter. By this time the girl, who is in her teens, has already chosen certain goals and guiding principles which clash with the parental expectations. The result is a conflict between the two generations.

Madhu came through as a person with ego strength and conviction. These traits perhaps made her unsuitable for a family set-up where conformity to sex role stereotyped behaviour was expected. Her attempts to be individualistic and autonomous were apparently not acceptable to her parents and this led to intergenerational tension. However, the turmoild did not lead to a state of identity confusion in Madhu. She knew the goals she was working towards and had confidence in her ability to achieve them.

12

Differences between Girls in Punjab and Uttar Pradesh

Since the rural sample was made up of girls from the villages of Punjab and Uttar Pradesh, the regional differences are also of interest.

It was found that on most variables there were no major differences. However, in general it was felt that the girls in U.P. were socialised with greater sternness. In U.P. there was emphasis on the adolescent girl not leaving the house without parental permission. A young girl walking alone in village Ismail Ganj was a rare sight. Although the nearest city, Lucknow, was only 8 kms. form the village, many girls had never visited the city; a few had been there two or three times in their life time.

In Punjab too, the girls were expected to observe some restraints. Parents and brothers often chided the girls if they went out to a friend's house. However, there was greater physical mobility among them. The girls in Punjab were engaged in one or more activities that involved leaving the home such as, going to school, to the fields for work, or to the nearest city to buy some materials for embroidery etc. They could traverse short distances within the village without being considered immodest. In fact, those from middle SES homes were allowed to visit Gurdaspur, the nearest city with a friend or a family member. Most of the lower SES girls in Punjab were wage labourers and hence had to work in the fields for practically the whole day. There were indicators of greater orthodoxy among families in U.P. while most girls in Punjab did not go to school for reasons of poverty, many in U.P. stated that schooling was not necessary for girls.

With regard to the treatment of the menstruating girl also there was a difference. While taboos related to participation of girls in ritual worship were equally strong in both states, the restrictions related to handling of food and segregation of the girl were much more stringent in U.P. The practice of total segregation of the girl was absent among the Punjab families. However, six girl from U.P. reported that they observed separation from other members of the family and dissociation from normal activities during menstruation. They could not enter the main house or the kitchen at that time.

The taboos related to cooking and handling of food during menstrual periods was reported by 27 out of 30 girls in U.P. In Punjab there were restrictions on handling pickles and preserves, and on consuming 'cold' foods. But, by and large, cooking and serving of food during menstrual periods was not prohibited.

The girls in Punjab gave some evidence of having partial control over their life decisions. Nine girls of the middle SES felt that they had some control over the decisions regarding marriage. Two girls perceived 'sufficient' control in this matter. In contrast, all the girls in U.P. perceived 'no control' over the circumstances leading to their own marriages. On the same lines, 10 girls from the middle SES in Punjab felt that they had some voice in their parents' choice of a marriage partner for them. In U.P. only one out of the eight unmarried girls gave this response.

Among the 60 rural subjects, 14 were married, and all belonged to U.P.; four were from the middle SES and 10 from the lower SES. In the Punjab sample, no girl was married, and this must be seen as a sub cultural difference. This indicated that early marriage was not a common feature in Punjab. In fact, the girls who worked as farm labour in Punjab shared the major financial burden of the family.

13

Summing Up

The major concern in this research was the identity of the Indian adolescent girl. Identity was studied in relation to the girl's role and status as a female, rather than to her core sense of self. There were two main reasons for such an emphasis in this study. One, cross cultural observations do not substantiate the argument held in traditional theories of psychology that individual autonomy is a necessary corollary of maturity. Recent studies on alternatives in psychological theorising (Anandalakshmy, 1981; Roland, 1982; Ramanujam, 1981; Marriott, 1982) have found that group coherence and conformity are highly valued in many cultures, including the Indian. When individual autonomy or excessive individualisation is seen as a counterforce to group allegiance, it is discouraged. Thus an Indian girl's identity is deeply intertwined with the social roles assigned to her. Secondly, the state of identity diffusion and crisis generally attributed to the period of adolescence in the technologically advanced Western cultures is not a characteristic of the adolescents growing up in India (Ramanujam, 1979).

In traditional India, the individual is seen primarily as a member of a certain language and religious group, hailing from a particular community, *Jati* and family. Actions and roles are interpreted in the light of the family's circumstances and reputation. Individual initiative and decisions are acceptable as long as they do not disturb the family bonds and conformity to expected behaviour is commended. Deviation from the norm is generally subject to scorn or at least to disapproval.

Since the Indian girl is part of a culture in which being group oriented is rewarded, her identity finds expression in non individualistic forms. It is rooted in her femininity. As acceptance of the traditional sex role is a cultural expectations, the attitude to and acceptance of the assigned role serve as fairly good indicators of identity.

The stress on group loyalty certainly undermines the significance of individual needs. However, this does not mean that individual differences are not recognized in the Indian world-view. The Hindu approach towards human experience is summed up in the belief in individual *Karma*, a concept which states that each soul carries a history of experience and action from earlier births. This predisposes an individual to certain specific actions. This notion may seem to reduce the emphasis on personal efficacy, but it respects the individual variations in maturation, endowments and abilities. "The child is perceived as an individual *atma* with his own *Karma* to live out" (Anandalakshmy, 1981 P.7).

In Western theories of this century, the human being is recognised as having a body and a mind, while in Indian metaphysical thinking, he not only has body and mind but also a soul (*atma*). The *atma* is regarded as immortal, as entity that originates from *Parmatma* (the Supreme), goes through repeated cycles of birth, growth and death until, after many lives, it attains *mukti* (release) from this cycle and finally unites with *Parmatma*.

In Western thinking, the term individual is used in a way that it denotes "a universal need to perceive oneself as somehow separate from others, no matter how much one may share motives, values and interests with others" (Conger, 1977, P.91). The Indian world view there is a constant exchange between the person and ecology, conscious and unconscious, past and present, self and society. In an unusual paper on Open Person and Fluid Family the anthropologist Marriott (1982) posited a unique theory that a person is 'dividual' (that which is divisible) and not 'individual' (that which is not divisible). He suggested that there are flows from one person to another, constituting the 'fluidarity' of the family. While one may not accept Marriott's thesis as the final statement on personhood in India - his perspective does make intuitive sense.

The process of individuation is subsumed in the concept of achievement of a sense of identity. Throughout his commentary on identity Erikson (1968, 1975 {c}) has assumed that the adolescent begins to function on his own volition. In other words, the adolescent is treated as a person who will have to take independent decisions regarding his or her future. This process implies a value for becoming independent and individualistic.

The Indian adolescent's identity formation takes place without the experiences of psychological adolescence. Identification with the sex role and acceptance of the socially ascribed status provide the groundwork for a sense of identity.

The second reason for the study of the girl in relation to her sex-role was an anticipated absence of a classical psychosocial moratorium among the rural and lower class adolescent girls.

According to Erikson, this bridge period precedes "psychosexual capacity for intimacy" and "psychosocial readiness for parenthood" (1968) and hence is a prerequisite to the completion of the process of identity formation. When one scrutinizes the definition of this interim period, the question of its cultural relevance becomes pertinent. He elaborates the concept of psychosocial moratorium, as "a delay of adult commitments and yet it is not a delay. It is a period that is characterized by a selective permissiveness on the part of youth, and yet it also often leads to deep, if often transitory, commitment on the part of youth, and ends in a more or less ceremonial confirmation of commitment on the part of society" (1968 P.157).

However, in the traditional Indian society, instead of a delay in adult role-commitment, there is an early and almost compulsory conformation of adult roles. Moreover there are stringent rules and regulations regarding role behaviour in contrast to societal permissiveness. Under these conditions, the psychosocial moratorium does not take place in the Indian adolescent's life, except in the lives of those who are upper class and urban, studying in formal educational institutions. Physical and physiological changes of puberty are a reality to all adolescents. However, most Indian adolescents are not 'adolescing' psychosocially. Future occupations are generally specified and choice of any kind within the system is limited. They do not encounter personal conflicts in choosing between meaningful alternative goals and the uncertainty of the adult roles ahead.

Erikson's epigenetic model presupposes that conflicts appropriate to the stage of adolescence that culminate in an identity crisis, should be resolved before a sense of identity is achieved. In the Indian context, on the basis of study of individual cases, Ramanujam (1979) observed that the lack of acknowledgment of adolescence as a distinct developmental phase in the culture has implications for adult life. In his paper Problems of Identity seen in the Indian Clinical Setting (1979) he remarked that "The psychological problems which, from Western orientation, should be resolved by an individual during adolescence, spill over into his adult life" (P.49). In other words, the resolution of adolescent conflicts is taken into adulthood and slows down the achievement of adult maturity.

The fact that adolescent girls adjust to circumstance rather than have a choice takes away the element of crisis. And if identity crisis is seen as the "psychosocial aspect of adolescing" (Erikson, 1968) there is no adolescence. The absence of crisis at adolescence is what makes the psychological adolescence less possible. Perhaps, as Ramanujam maintains, the conflicts appear in adulthood.

The differences among the groups on traditionality were found to be statistically significant in the present study. This implied that socio-economic status and place of residence were crucial variables affecting traditionality. Being rural and lower class was associated with a high level of traditionality while being urban and upper class connoted a low level of traditionality.

The lower SES girls (both rural and urban) were found to be fairly well adjusted in their socially defined roles having accepted them as destined. The urban upper SES girls adapted themselves satisfactorily to the demands of the role expected of them, the sex role itself being defined slightly differently for them. The middle SES girls of both rural and urban groups were found to experience problems in the process of identification with their sex role. While the rural girl conveyed a feeling of powerlessness in her female role, her urban counterpart experienced a distance from the culturally prescribed role, identifying the least with it as compared to girls in the other groups. The middle SES groups were significantly more traditional than the upper SES group, and yet they were lower on the variable of sex role identification.

Thus the relationship between the level of traditionality and the degree of identification with the expected sex role was curvilinear. The antecedents of such a relationship were multifarious, some discernible and some not. Of the more perceptible factors, formal education emerged as the single most important factor. Related were other correlates such as need for achievement, sense of power and control, attitude to discrimination between sexes, and degree of satisfaction with the sex role. The level of education was positively related with social class.

The assumption here, of course, is not that education *per se* is a sufficient factor in producing the given consequences. The level of education that a girl will be allowed to reach is determined by her social class, to a large extent. Thus it would be rare to find a girl with a university degree in a lower SES sample, or an illiterate girl in an upper SES group.

In the present investigation, when the sociological circumstances were more or less constant, the more educated girls tended to view their environment as restrictive and non conducive to personal development than the less educated or illiterate girls. Apparently those who had been to school upto eighth standard or more, i.e., during their preadolescent and adolescent years, experienced the impact of schooling more definitively than others. The impact was in the form of awareness, and need for self-expression and recognition.

An interesting way in which education seemed to have played its role was through revealing to these girls the vast differences in the socialisation of boys and girls, brothers and sisters. A girl who is never sent to school may accept the inferiority of her sex and grow up in awe of her brothers. Their other-ness is reinforced by the fact that what they do is rarely questioned.

The situation for the school going girl was different. She went to school like her brother but unlike him was not to go anywhere else.

She was expected to help in the house and had to stop going to school when the family demanded it. The implications for the girl were that she was as capable as a boy but not as free. If the girls attended school even for a few years, they became quite aware of the extra opportunities the boys enjoyed partly as a function of attending an institution. When equated with school going boys the girls began to realise their disadvantageous position as females.

In his study LeVine (1980) also found that formal education helped a girl in "overcoming her reticence to speak as an adult, inducing her to display what she knows and thinks for public evaluation, and encouraging her to view her assertions and attention seeking tendencies as positive aspects of her self rather than as breaches of etiquette"(P.81).

If schooling means some form of training in assertiveness, then additional years of schooling would mean more practice in self assertion and increased confidence in one's own ability to control circumstances. In general the more educated girls, who were also middle and upper SES subjects, gave increasingly greater evidence of free expression of opinions and awareness of opportunities. However, that is where the similarity between the two SES groups ends. The socialisation climate of the upper SES girl permitted her a moderate degree of freedom to be autonomous and to 'transgress' the code of feminine behaviour within limits. The grudges that she held against her parents and the resentment of societal moves appeared more like philosophic conflicts of an emerging adult rather than as concrete problems.

Compared to her, the middle SES girl (whether rural or urban) was in a predicament. She had been allowed to acquire some degree of education (the specific period being dependent on a number of factors) because literacy is a value even for her marriage. A similar reason for the increase in the number of educated young girls was observed by Mandelbaum (1972). Ideally, the education of a person should promote ideas of independence, egalitarianism, self expression, reasoning and achievement orientation with competitiveness being an inseparable part of the experience of schooling.

Assuming that the education of the middle SES girls was nowhere near ideal, it can at least be expected that schooling would have acquainted the girls with some of these concepts. The school thus represented their entry into a world of values that were not compatible with those of the demands of the sex role. Schooling apparently produced a dilemma for the girl in the middle SES. She encountered the contradiction of having to value education but not being allowed to utilise it. Indeed the process of reconciling these opposing trends has its repurcussions. The educated middle class girl seemed to reject both, the traditional boundaries limiting her sphere of activity, and the taboos that inhibited normal self expression.

On first glance, there appeared to be a considerable difference in the amount of freedom permitted to girls in different groups, the rural lower SES group and the urban SES group being at the lower and upper ends of this continuum respectively. However, due to the contrast effect, in which one group was seen against the other, the differences appeared magnified. Thus the amount of freedom enjoyed by the girls in the upper SES group seemed tremendous as compared to that of lower and middle SES girls.

Yet when compared with the degree of autonomy of adolescent girls in some other cultures, e.g. the sexual freedom of the girl in Samoa (Margaret Mead's study), or the economic and interpersonal independence of the American girl, the Indian upper SES girl's freedom seemed to be quite limited. In general, she grew up under the close supervision of her parents until she was married. She was dependent for financial and moral support on her parents to complete her education. Heterosexual mixing of peers was minimal and mainly a status symbol - very different from the American girl's dating behaviour. The marriage partners were selected by parents and the girl's preference for a career was not given serious thought by their families.

Across the entire sample studied, it was found that in general, the girls had internalised the male bias in the culture. They also accepted prescriptions of restrictions on girls. Equality between sexes was not expected as a matter of right by the girls, except in the upper SES group. Even they interpreted equality in socially accepted term. Despite several inter-SES and rural-urban differences, the predominant value for the male emerged very clearly.

The analysis of the adolescent girl's identity in this chapter lends confirmation to the argument put forward in Introduction that the traditional person has a sense of security. The lower SES girl, who was the most traditional of the three SES groups, appeared to find her security in the familiar cultural rules and regulations, customs and folkways, and clear sex role expectations. However, decreasing traditionality was not related to a lowered sense of security. The upper SES girl, though least traditional, also had a sense of security. The pillars of her support were her education, the opportunity to develop personal abilities, a near equal status with boys in the family and her parents' social and professional status. Each of these factors complemented the others. Together they enhanced her confidence in herself.

The middle SES girl, though moderately traditional, showed signs of uncertainty in her bearing. She had formal education as well as the drive to go ahead. But she lacked support from the status of the family which was naturally 'middle class'. Her formal education had taught her to value equality, but her socialisation experience was of preferential treatment to boys. In her group, working to earn a living was treated by girls as a natural step after schooling. But this was thwarted by the scarcity of jobs for that educational level. In brief, the middle SES girl was confronted with conflicting experiences that probably produced a sense of insecurity.

One might put the Indian girl on two hypothetical continua : one depicting the complexity of culture from low to high, and the other representing the stability of role from high to low. Hypothetically, the first continuum should be negatively related with the second one.

Complexity of Culture

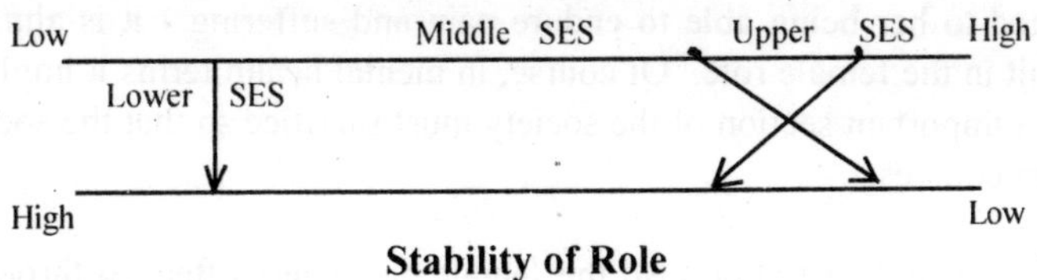

Stability of Role

Figure 3. Positions of SES groups on two hypothetical continua.

Figure 3 illustrates that SES is a significant variable determining the place of the Indian girl on these continua.

The lower SES girl was the lowest on 'Complexity of culture'. Her life style was simpler than that of the middle and the upper SES girl and gave evidence of a stable role. The middle SES girl was lowest on 'Stablity of role' as she experienced the greatest amount of confusion of values and goals. The upper SES girl revealed a stablity achieved under instability- inducing circumstances. On the 'Complexity of culture' continuum both middle and upper SES girls were in close proximity with the environment becoming progressively more complex from middle to upper SES.

In the Indian literary sources that were reviewed earlier, a whole range of characteristics of adolescent girls had emerged. In general, however, the typical girl was gentle, responsible, obedient, and self effacing. The findings of this study provide empirical evidence for this type. The girl between 16-19 years was unassertive, responsible and compliant. She had internalized parental values and expectations as her own. The constraints and restrictions, though resented at a personal level, were accepted as something that could not be negotiated. Taboos and traditions were very much a part of her life. In comparison to a boy, an Indian girl seemed to have much less freedom of thought and activity.

For an outside observer, the Indian girl might be an object of pity. An observer who has grown up in the same culture would sympathise with her, but would also understand the reason for her strength despite her status. He or she would know that in the Indian context some element of suffering is associated with being a woman. There is a value attached to her being able to endure pain and suffering - it is almost in-built in the female role. Of course, in mental health terms it implies that an important section of the society must sacrifice so that the social system coheres.

In Indian fiction also the female characters often go through hardships and anguish due to the fact that they are women (Anand, 1970; Anand, undated; Bedi, 1967; Bhattacharya, 1978, Pritam, 1973; Sobti, 1972). In other words, growing up with the acceptance of a secondary place in relation of the male is conducive for satisfactory adjustment to the social set up. Envy of the male position by females is tolerated as long as it does not actually disturb the status quo. The identity of the adolescent girl includes her awareness of this reality.

It was this awareness that helped her to tolerate the experience of being treated as a lesser individual. Her activities were group oriented, her ideal was group coherence and her motto for conduct was modesty. However, formal education seemed to give her an impetus to question the social system, specially the restrictions on her self-expression.

The only major way in which the image of the girl as reflected in this study was different from the image in the literary sources was related to her role as a working girl. While in the literature the girl was, in general, seen to be confined to the home, the average girl in the study worked outside the home or wished to do so in order to satisfy her personal and economic needs.

Formal education seemed to play a significant role in this area. Even if a girl had a few years of education, she desired a 'respectable' occupation such as that of a teacher or a clerk. Although a few rural girls were working as labourers on daily wages, they did not equate this with employment. They aspired for salaried jobs, a possibility that was unrealistic. They were not aware of the scarcity of jobs for women with low levels of education. They had also not taken into account the social disapproval the family would have to face if the girl was allowed to work with unknown employers. Nevertheless, this finding was a significant indicator of a new fact of the adolescent girl in India.

When compared with Erikson's model of an adolescent in the West, the Indian girl did not face an identity crisis during her adolescence. The development of her individual personality was encompassed within cultural expectations and role requirements. These helped to absorb her personal crises, and she could find fulfilment and recognition within the expected roles.

14

The Emerging Paradigm

A model of the identity of the Indian adolescent girl that emerges reflects that socio-cultural and demographic factors are critical to its shape and content. Psychological aspects seem to be overshadowed by the social experience.

The model (Figure 4) reflects the social reality where gender identity is primary. In general, the lower the SES level, the earlier is the girl's initiation into household work. Within a particular social class, traditional families train their daughters early in household responsibilities. By the age of 19 years all young women acquire a number of skills in running a household. At the psychological level this training also involves inculcating traditional values of the family and observing the prescribed restraint in individualized expression. At the end of the stage of adolescence the girl's sense of sex role identity is not diffused : it is perhaps prematurely crystallised. Her ego-identity is not separate from her gender identity.

The girl's identity is also influenced by the level of her formal education. While the level of education is predictably related to her socio-economic level, its effect is most clearly seen when girls of the same group are compared. Just a few years of schooling appears to be instrumental in evoking thoughts regarding self worth and aspirations for the future. These may be unrealistic within the cultural milieu. However, education does not overwhelm the girl's sense of identification with her gender role. Even if she aspires to be 'well' educated, she

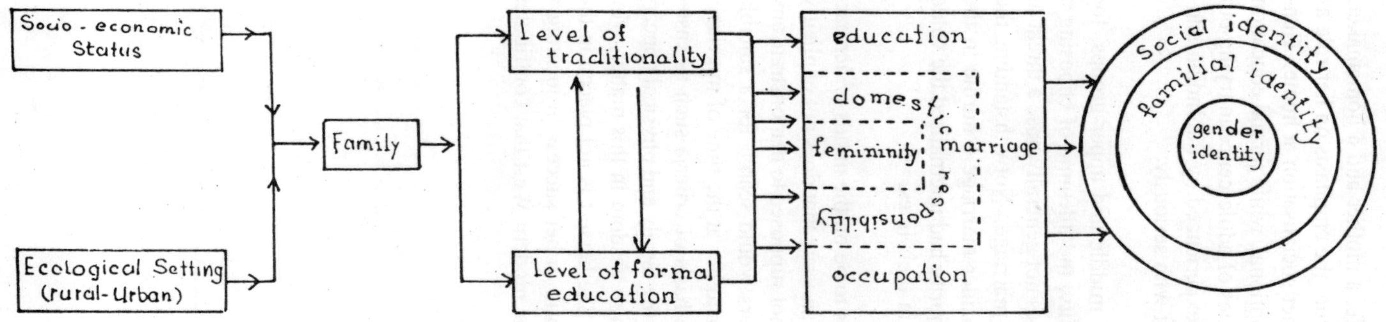

Figure 4. Sex-role identity as influenced by social and cultural variables.

Note : The socio-economic status and the ecological setting of the family influence the levels of traditionality and formal education of its memebers. The adolescent girl's level of traditionality is influenced by her formal education. The interaction of these factors determines the girl's feminine identity, of which domestic responsibilities and marriage are essential aspects, education and occupation being optional. In the final analysis the girl's gender identity is encompassed within her familial and social identity.

also plans, at the same time, to be a wife, a mother and a homemaker. Throughout the period of formal education, the emphasis on her role as a future homemaker continues through her socialisation at home. Gender role appropriate socialisation is not optional, while formal education is. It therefore follows that the vicissitudes of adolescence in trying out several roles (Erikson's model) are not experienced by the Indian adolescent : there are no roles to experiment with seriously.

Even the girls from the urban middle and upper groups, for whom higher education is a part of reality, the dilemma of choosing a specific course in education or career does not generally pose a threat to their faith in the traditional goal, that is, marriage. Notwithstanding the sporadic attempts of a few girls to consider marriage a hurdle in the achievement of their goals, the large majority had internalised the value for marriage as an inevitable milestone in their lives.

While the girl's marriage seems to be on the minds of her parents even before she comes of age, it is an issue that does not explicitly concern the girl herself. At least, she is not supposed to demonstrate any obvious interest. The parents and others would search for a suitable partner for her, who might be a stranger to her at the time of marriage. His suitability would be defined on the basis of criteria such as caste, socio economic status, the reputation of the family and physical appearance. The girl places faith in her parents' wisdom in this matter, who she feels, will do what is best for her. She herself is not placed in the predicament of establishing her self worth in her success in locating a life partner. This is an experience in the modern West that contributes to the crisis of identity.

REFERENCES

Aaron, P.G. ; Marihal, M.G. & Maltesha, R.N. (1969) A common socio economic status scale for rural and urban areas. *Research Monograph*, **3**. Karnataka University, Dharwar.

Adelson, J. (1979). *Psychology Today*, Feb. 33-38..

Anand, M.R. *(undated)Two leaves and a bud.* New Delhi : Orient.

Anand, M.R. (1954).*The Village*. New Delhi : Orient.

Anand, M.R. (1970).*Untouchable*. New Delhi : Orient.

Anandalakshmy, S. (1973). The process of modernization: perspectives from India. Paper presented at conference The *interface of Culture and Learning*, East West Centre, Honolulu, Hawaii, Jan. 29 - Feb.3

Anandalakshmy, S. (1975).Socialisation for competence. In J.N. Berry & W.J. Lonner (Eds.) *Applied Cross cultural psychology*. The Netherlands : Swetz & Zeitlinger.

Anandalakshmy, S. (1981).Learning to live in families : Speculations on the holographic image of the Indian. Paper presented at the second workshop of *The Person in South Asia Project* : *Life Courses and Family Relationships in Alternative Psychologies of South Asia*, Chicago, Sept.6-8.

Anandalakshmy, S.(Ed.) (1994). *The girl child and the family : An action research study*. Dept. of Women and Child Development, Ministry of HRD, Govt. of India, New Delhi.

Armer, M.(1970). Formal education and psychological malaise in an African society. *Sociology of Education*. 43, 143-158.

Bajaj, D. (1990). *Perceptions of being female among urban school going adolescent girls*, Unpublished master's dissertation, University of Delhi.

Bajaj R. (1973). *Patterns of socialization for competence in Harijan families in a New Delhi slum.* Unpublished master's dissertation, University of Delhi.

Bakan, D.(1975). Adolescence in America : from idea to social fact. In C.J. Guardo (Ed.), *The adolescent as individual : Issues and insights.* New York : Harper & Row.

Bandura, A. (1975). The stormy decade : fact or fiction. In C.J. Guardo (Ed.), *The adolescent as individual : Issues and insights.* New York : Harper & Row.

Bawa, R. (1972). *Socialisation for competence and its relation to achievement attidues in preadolescent children in the Sikh group in Delhi.* Unpublished master's dissertation, University of Delhi.

Bedi, R.S. (1967). [I take this woman] {K. Singh trans.}. New Delhi : Orient.

Benedek, E.P. (1979).Dilemmas in research on female adolescent development. In M. Sugar (Ed.), *Female adolescent development* New York : Brunner/Mazel.

Bhattacharya, B. (1952). *Music for Mohini.* New Delhi : Orient.

Bhattacharya, B. (1955). *He who rides a tiger.* New Delhi : Orient.

Bhattacharya, B. (1966). *Shadow from Ladakh.* New Delhi : Orient.

Bhattacharya, B. (1978). *So many hungers.* New Delhi : Orient.

Binepal, G. (1980). *Peer status of XI standard girls : Selected Correlates.* Unpublished master's dissertation, University of Delhi.

Bronson, G.W. (1959). Identity diffusion in late adolescents. *The Journal of Abnormal and Social Psychology*, **59**, 414-417.

Carpenter, W.W. (1975). Identity development and adjustment of lower socio-economic adolescents. *Dissertation Abstracts International,* **35**, 6088-6089.

Clarke, E. & Ruble, D.N. (1978). Young adolescents' beliefs concerning menstruation. *Child Development,* 49, 231-234.

Conger, J.J. (1977). *Adolescence and Youth.* New York : Harper & Row.

Constantinople, A.(1975). An Eriksonian measure of personality development in college students. In C.J. Guardo (Ed.), *The adolescent as individual : Issues and insights.* New York : Harper & Row.

Cormack, M.(1961(a)). *She who rides a peacock.* New Delhi : Asia Publishing House.

Cormack, M.(1961(b)). *The Hindu woman.* New Delhi : Asia Publishing House.

Das, V. (1979). Reflections on the social construction of adulthood. In S. Kakar (Ed.), *Identity and adulthood.* Delhi : Oxford.

Desai, A. (1980). *Cry, the peacock.* New Delhi, Orient.

Dhingra, N. (1988). *Peer acceptance among adolescent boys and girls : An action research.* Unpublished master's dissertation, University of Delhi.

Douvan, E. & Adelson, J. (1966). *The adolescent experience.* New York : John Wiley.

Dube, S.C. (1967). *Indian Village.* New York : Harper & Row.

Erikson, E.H. (1958). *Young man Luther.* Landon : Faber & Faber.

Erikson, E.H. (1968). *Identity : Youth and crisis.* London : Faber & Faber.

Erikson, E.H. (1975 (a)). *Dimensions of a new identity.* New Delhi : Light Life Publishers.

Erikson, E.H. (1975 (b)). Adolescence as unprootedness. In C.J. Guardo (Ed.), *The adolescent as individual : Issues and insights.* New York : Harper & Row.

Erikson, E.H. (1975 (c)). *Life history and the historical moment.* New York : Norton,

Ganguly, S.N. (1977). *Tradition, modernity and development.* Delhi : Macmillan.

George, E.(1973). *A study of the patterns of socialization for competence of Harijan boys and girls in a Delhi village.* Unpublished master's dissertation, University of Delhi.

Gill, H.S. (1977). *A phulkari from Bhatinda. Patiala* : Punjabi University.

Gill, P.(1987). *Adolescent perceptions of sex role stereotypes in areas of education and employment.* Unpublished matster's dissertation, University of Delhi.

Gill, R. (1974). *Patterns of socialization for competence in potters' families in New Delhi.* Unpublished master's dissertation, University of Delhi.

Gilligan, C. (1982). *In a different voice : Psychological theory and women's develoment.* Cambridge : Harvard University Press.

Glenn, N.D; Alston, J.P. & Weiner, D.(1970). *Social startification : A research bibliography.* Berkely : Glendessary Press.

Gulati, M. (1980). *Peer status, self concept and parental interaction among 10th std. girls.* Unpublished master's dissertation, University of Delhi.

Gupta, A. (1988). *Orientation and self perception of Mehendiwali girls.* Unpublished master's dissertation, University of Delhi.

Hate, C.A. (1969). *Changing status of woman.* Bombay : Allied Publishers.

Horney, K. (1973). The problem of feminine masochism. In J.B. Miller (Ed.), *Psychonanalysis and women.* Maryland : Penguin.

Inkeles, A. & Smith, D.H. (1974). *Becoming modern.* Cambridge : Harvard University Press.

Islam, N. (1976). *Self concept and peer acceptance in pre adolescent* school going girls. Unpublished master's dissertation, University of Delhi.

Jacobson, D. & Wadley, S.S., (1977). *Women in India : Two perspectives.* New Delhi : Manohar.

Jhabvala, R.P. (1956). *The nature of passion.* London : Allen & Unwin.

Kahl, J.A. (1968). *The measurement of modernism : a study of values in Brazil and Mexico.* London : University of Texas Press.

Kakar, S. (1978). *The inner world.* Delhi : Oxford.

Kapur, P. (1974). *The changing status of the working woman in India.* Delhi : Vikas.

Kapur, P. (1976). *Love, marriage and sex and the Indian woman.* New Delhi : Orient.

Khanna, G. & Verghese, M.A. (1978). *Indian women today.* New Delhi : Vikas.

Khosla, N. (1982). *Self concept of the adolescent girl : selected correlates.* Unpublished master's dissertation, University of Delhi.

Konopka, G. (1976). *Young girls : a portrait of adolescence.* New Jersey : Prentice Hall.

Kumar, A. (1980). *Peer relationships and familial dynamics among school going girls.* Unpublished master's dissertation, University of Delhi.

Kumari, R.; Singh, R. & Dubey, A. (1990). *Growing up in rural India : problems and needs of adolescent girls.* New Delhi : Radiant Publishers.

Kuppuswamy, B. (1962). *Socio economic status scale (urban)* Delhi : Manasayan.

Lavoie,J.C. (1976). Ego identity formation in middle adolescence. *Journal of Youth and Adolescence*, 5, 283-300.

Lerner, D. (1958).*The passing of traditional society.* Glencoe, Ill. : Free Press.

LeVine, R.A. (1980). Influence of women's schooling on maternal behaviour in the Third World. *Comparative Education Review Supplement.* 78-105.

Maccoby, E.E. & Jacklin, O.N. (1975). *The psychology of sex differences.* London : Oxford.

Madan, T.N. (1965). *Family and kinship.* New Delhi : Asia Publishing House.

Makhija, V. (1981). *Sex role stereotypes among 16 years old adolescents.* Unpublished master's dissertation, University of Delhi.

Mandelbaum, D.G. (1972). *Society in India.* Bombay : Popular prakashan.

Marcia, J.E. (1975). Development and validation of ego identity status. In C.J. Guardo (Ed.), *The adolescent as individual : Issues and insights.* New York : Harper & Row.

Marcia, J.E. & Friedman, M.L. (1975). Ego identity of college women. In C.J. Guardo (Ed.), *The adolescent as individual : Issues and insights.* New York : Harper & Row.

Markandaya, K. (1973). *Two virigins.* New Delhi : Vikas.

Markandaya, K. (1980). *Nectar in a siere.* Delhi : Jaico Publishing House.

Marriott, M. (1982). Open person and fluid family. Unpublished presentation at the conference *Workshop on Healing, Personal Transformation and the Life Course in India.* Project on Human Potential. Harvard University, GSE, June 14-19.

Mathai, P. (1972). *Relation between independence training and acheivement attitudes in preadolescent children in the Syrian Christian community in Delhi.* Unpublished master's dissertation, University of Delhi.

Mathew, A. (1960). Expectations of college students regarding their marriage. *Journal of Family Welfare,* 12(3), March

Mead, M. (1939). Coming of age in Samoa. In M. Mead, *From the South Seas.* New York : William Morrow.

Mehta, R. (1977). *Inside the haveli.* New Delhi: Arnold-Heinemann.

Menon, L. (1976). *Adoelscents' perceptions of the experience of pubescence.* Unpublished master's dissertation, University of Delhi.

Minturn, L. & Hitchcock, J.T. (1963). The Rajputs of Khalapur, India. In B.B. Whiting (Ed.) *Six cultures; studies of child rearing.* New York : John Wiley.

Murthy, V. (1974). *Patterns of socialization for competence in the families of toy makers of Muhammadpur, New Delhi.* Unpublished master's dissertation, University of Delhi.

Nangia, A. (1981). *A study of certin factors affecting the age of onset of menstruation and the associated symptoms in girls aged 15-18 years.* Unpublished master's dissertation, University of Delhi.

Nandy, A. & Kakar, S. (1980). Culture and personality. In U. Pareek

(Ed.), *A survey of research in psychology (1971-76)*. Bombay : Popular Prakashan.

National Institute of Public Cooperation and Child Development. (1980). *Country report on child development in India : Implications for policy and training*. New York : Author.

Nischal, R. (1987). *School performance and family dynamics : The case of high and low performers (15-17 year old girls) in a government school*. Unpublished master's dissertation, University of Delhi.

Offer, D. (1969). *The psychological world of the teenager*. New York : Basic Books.

Pant, I. (1981). *A study of certain factors affecting the age of onset of menstruation and the associated symptoms in girls aged 12-15 years*. Unpublished master's dissertation, University of Delhi.

Paranjpe, A.C. (1975). *In search of identity*. Delhi : Macmillan.

Pareek, U. & Trivedi, G. (1964). *Socio economic status scale (rural)*. Delhi : Manasayan.

Podd, M.H. (1972). Ego identity status and morality : the relationship between two developmental constructs. *Developmental Psychology*, **6**, 497-507.

Portes, A. (1973). The factorial structure of modernity : empirical replication and a critique. *American Journal of Sociology*, 79(1), 15-44.

Pritam, A. (1973). Ganje Ki Kali. In *Amrita Pritam ki shreshtha rachanayen*. New Delhi : Bhartiya Jnanpith.

Pritam, A. (1973). Jungli Buti. In *Amrita Pritam ki shreshtha rachanayen*. New Delhi : Bhartiya Jnanpith.

Pritam, A. Pinjar. (1973). In *Amrita Pritam ki shreshtha rachanayen*. New Delhi : Bhartiya Jnanpith.

Ramanujam, B.K. (1979). Toward maturity : problems of identity seen in the Indian clinical setting. In S. Kakar (Ed.), *Identity and adulthood.* Delhi : Oxford.

Ramanujam, B.K. (1981). Clinical case studies. Paper presented at the second workshop of *The Person in South Asia Project : Life Courses and Family Relationships in Alternative Psychologies of South Asia,* Chicago, Sept. 6-8.

Ranade, S.N. & Ramachandran, P. (1970). *Women and employment.* Bombay.

Randhawa, M.S. (1959). *Basholi Painting.* Publication Division, Ministry of Information and Broadcasting, Government of India. New Delhi.

Rasmussen, J. (1964). Relationship of ego identity to psychological effectiveness. *Psychol. Reports.* 15, 815-825.

Registrar General and Census commissioner, India. (1981). *Census of India,* New Delhi : author

Roland, A. (1982). The transcendent - immanent self : continuity and counterpoint to the familiar self. Paper presented at the conference *Workshop on Healing, Personal Transformation and the Life Course in India,* Project on Human Potential. Harvard University, Graduate school of Education, June 14-19.

Ross, A.D. (1961). *Hindu family in its urban setting.* Canada : University of Toronto Press.

Sahai, A. (1974). *Patterns of socialization for competence in families of craftsmen : mat makers in New Delhi* : Unpublished master's dissertation, University of Delhi.

Saraf, J. (1972). *Socialization for independence and its relation to achievement attitudes in preadolescent children in a Rajasthani ethnic group.* Unpublished master's dissertation, University of Delhi.

Sareen, S. (1981). *Sex role stereotypes among 13-year-old adolescents.* Unpublished master's dissertation, University of Delhi.

Schnaiberg, A. (1970[a]), Rural Urban residence and modernism : a study of Ankara Province, Turkey. *Demography*. 7 (1), 71-85.
Schnaiberg, A. (1970(b)), Measuring modernism; theoretical and empirical explorations. *American Journal of Sociology*, **76**(3), 399-425.

Sethi, R. (1976). *Modernization of working women in developing society*. New Delhi : National Publishing House.

Sheth, J. (1972). A matter of arrangement. *Times of India Weekly, Sunday Magazine*, March.

Shils, E. (1971). Tradition. In A.R. Desai (Ed.), *Modernization of underdeveloped societies*. Bombay : Thacker.

Shirpurkar, G.R. (1967). Construction and standardization of a scale for measuring socio economic status of farm families. *Indian Journal of Extension Education*, **3**(1-2), 16-24.

Shopper, M. (1979). The (re) discovery of the vagina and the importance of the menstrual tampon. In M. Sugar (Ed.), *Female adolescent development*. New York : Brunner/Mazel.

Singh, A.M. (1975). The study of women in India : some problems in methodology. In A. de'Souza (Ed.), *Women in contemporary India*. New Delhi : Indian Social Institute.

Smith, D.H. & Inkeles, A. (1966). The OM Scale : a comparative socio psychological measure of individual mdoernity. *Sociometry, 29*, 353-377.

Sobti, K. (1972). *Dar Se bichhudi*. Delhi : Rajkamal.

Sobti, K. (1979). [Blossoms in darkness] (K. Nagpal trans.). New Delhi : Vikas.

Srinivas, M.N. (1952). *Caste in modern India and other essays*. New York : Asia publishing House.

Tandon, D.K. (1988). *Growing up in a slum : A profile of adolescent girls,* Unpublished master's dissertation, University of Delhi.

Vasudev, M. (1974). *Patterns of socialization for competence in craft families involved in making lac-bangles.* Unpublished master's dissertation, University of Delhi.

Verma, N. (1974). *Lal teen ki Chhat.* Delhi : Rajkamal.

Vohra, A. (1973). *Patterns of socialization for competence in low income families in New Delhi.* Unpublished master's dissertation, University of Delhi.

Waterman, A.S. & Waterman, C.K. (1975). A longitudinal study of changes in ego identity status during the freshman year at College. In C.J. Guardo (Ed.), *The adolescent as individual : Issues and insights.* New York : Harper & Row.

Westley, W. & Elkin, F. (1969). The protective environment and adolescent socialization. In M. Gold & E. Douvan (Eds.), *Adolescent development : Readings in research and theory.* Boston : Allyn & Bacon.

Yardi, R. (1972). A *study of the differences in the patterns of socialization of rural boys and girls in a selected village near Delhi.* Unpublished master's dissertation, University of Delhi.

YMCA of India, (1971). *The educated woman in Indian society.* New Delhi : Tata McGraw Hill.

APPENDIX - I

ATTITUDES ON ISSUES OF SOCIAL SIGNIFICANCE

Respondent's Name : ....

The present scale consists of 35 items related to the common Indian social and familial issues. Each item is represented by part (a) and part (b) given in columns I and III respectively. In column II there are three squares A "In between", and B.

Before answering, read the part (a) and part (b) of each item first. Then decide, of the two statements, with which one do you agree, or come nearest to agreement. If it is part (a) then put a tick in the square A in column II, If you agree with part (b) then put a tick in the square B. If case you feel that you cannot agree with either of the two parts and prefer a mid-way course then tick the square "In-between".

Please answer all the items, your co-operation will be appreciated.

Item No.		I	II				III
Code			A	In between	B		
1 MSM	a) T	It is proper for a man to dominate over his wife in all major issues.	☐	☐	☐	b)	A man should treat his wife as an equal and consult her on all major issues.
2 F	a) M	When looking for a job, being near one's parents should not be an important consideration.	☐	☐	☐	b)	A son should find a job near his parents' place of residence.
3 CA	a) T	One should get married only within within one's caste	☐	☐	☐	b)	If suitable match is not found within the caste there is no harm in marrying into a different caste.
4 IBS	a)	The birth of a child should be greeted in the same way whether it is a son or a daughter	☐	☐	☐	b)	The birth of a son should be greeted with greater celebrations than the birth of a daughter.

Item No. / Code		I	II A	II In between	II B		III
5 Ft	a) T	It is good luck more than hard work that makes man successful.	☐	☐	☐	b)	Hard work is more important than luck for a man to achieve something in life.
6 AH	a) T	The older the person the more valuable and sound would be his ideas as compared to younger people.	☐	☐	☐	b)	Valuable and sound ideas can be produced by any one irrespective of age.
7 MP	a) T	At the time of a wedding in the family all near and distant relatives and friends should be invited	☐	☐	☐	b)	A wedding coremony should be performed only with the immediate family members attending it.
8 MDM	a) M	A wife should have the freedom to discuss her point of view with her husband instead of having to obey him blindly	☐	☐	☐	b)	It is a wife's duty to do what her husband tells her husband to do.
9 F	a) M	When in need help can be sought from either friends or relations whoever is easy to approach.	☐	☐	☐	b)	When in need a man should seek help from relatives only.
10 CA	a) T	A person from an upper caste should not accept food touched by a person from the lower caste.	☐	☐	☐	b)	Pollution of food is not caused by factors like caste of a person but by hygienic conditions under which it is cooked and served.

Item No. Code		I	II A	In between	B		III
11 IBS	a) M	A woman cannot be held responsible for the sex of her child	☐	☐	☐	b)	In order to be worthy of her family a woman should produce at least one son
12 Ft	a) T	Some people are able to bring harm and misfortune to others through magic.	☐	☐	☐	b)	Things that are explained as magical can probably be attributed to a reason that people prefer to avoid (i.e. lack of success)
13 AH	a) M	The opinion of elders need not always be sought. It depends on who has the information and wisdom - not on age.	☐	☐	☐	b)	Elders in the family should be consulted on all matters.
14 MP	a) T	Weddings should be celebrated with pomp and show.	☐	☐	☐	b)	Wedding should take place quietly and simply.
15 MSM	a) T	Women should have the opportunity to express their potential through various interests even if these are outside the home.	☐	☐	☐	b)	A woman should not have any interests other than the home and the children.
16 F	a) M	A grown up son should be allowed to decide whether he wants to continue his father's profession or not.	☐	☐	☐	b)	Even if the son does not like his father's profession, he should follow it.
17 CA	a) T	One should not trust people from other castes for financial dealings.	☐	☐	☐	b)	The caste of a person is not related to his trust worthiness in financial dealings.

Item No. Code		I	II A	II In between	II B		III
18 IBC	a) M	It is totally unethical for a man to remarry because his wife has not had a son.	☐	☐	☐	b)	A man should be allowed to remarry if his first wife has not produced a son.
19 Ft	a) M	It is wise to plan one's future even if some plans do not work out as foreseen.	☐	☐	☐	b)	There is no point in making future plans as what happens the next moment is not in one's own hands.
20 AH	a) T	Children should obey their parents unquestioningly and not ask for explanations.	☐	☐	☐	b)	Parents should not resent it if their children ask for reasons for what-ever they are asked to do.
21 MP	a) T	Parents should give dowry at their daughter's wedding.	☐	☐	☐	b)	The practice of giving dowry at a daughter's wedding should be dis-continued.
22 MSM	a) M	A man should help his wife in the house and in the care of children as and when necessary.	☐	☐	☐	b)	Household work is a woman's domain and her husband should not help in house work and care of children.
23 F	a) T	Social functions in the family should always be attended even if that means missing work/school/college for a few days.	☐	☐	☐	b)	Social functions in the family should be attended only as long as they do not interfere with the efficiency of work or attendence at school/college.

Item No. Code		I	II A	II In between	II B		III
24 CA	a) M	While casting ones vote in elections factors like caste should never influence one's choice.	☐	☐	☐	b)	When casting ones vote in elections a person should preferably vote for a candidate who belongs to his own caste.
25 IBS	a) T	Daughters should not expect to have a formal education and certainly not as much as sons.	☐	☐	☐	b)	Daughters and sons should have the same opportunity for the education of their choice.
26 Ft	a) T	Accidents cannot be avoided as these are due to bad luck.	☐	☐	☐	b)	Accidents can be avoided as frequently they are due to the carelessness of people.
27 AH	a) T	If there is a serious quarrel/argument between two persons, the younger person must give in first and apologize.	☐	☐	☐	b)	In a quarrel/argument whoever is in the wrong must apologize age has no relationship to seriousness of fault.
28 MP	a) M	Bridegrooms who demand or are a party to the family's demand for dowry from the prospective bride's family should be boycotted for marriage alliances.	☐	☐	☐	b)	The groom's family should be given the dowry that they demand if the boy is a good match for the girl.

Item No. Code		I	II A	II In between	II B		III
29 MSM	a) T	Even if she is unhappy it is a woman's duty to keep the marriage going rather than to want to be separated.	☐	☐	☐	b)	If a woman is very unhappy with her husband she should be allowed to seek a divorce.
30 F	a) M	After marriage sons should maintain their own independent units away from the parents' house.	☐	☐	☐	b)	A married son should live with his parents under all circumstances.
31 CA	a) M	A religious function should be open to people from all castes, lower or high.	☐	☐	☐	b)	In a religious function people from lower castes should not be allowed.
32 IBS	a) T	Greater control should be exercised onthe conduct of girls than of boys.	☐	☐	☐	b)	Sons and daughters should be brought up with the same amount of trust, control and freedom.
33 Ft	a) M	If a farmer repeatedly fails to get a good crop over many years it only means that he must change his farming methods.	☐	☐	☐	b)	If a farmer repeatedly fails to get a good crop over many years it is probably so because he had done wrong deeds for which he is being punished.
34 AH	a) T	Seniority is the best criterion for promotion to positions of authority.				b)	Efficiency and competence, not age, should be the basis of promotion.

Item No. Code		I	II A	II In between	II B		III
35 MP	a)	All the traditional rites and rituals of Hindu wedding have meaning and should be performed.	☐	☐	☐	b)	The time spent on marriage rites and rituals should be cut down to suit the modern pace of life.

Subject's remarks about the scale if any :-

APPENDIX II

Interview Schedule

Preliminary Data

Respondent :   Age :

Education :   Area of residence :

Father's / Husband's occupation :

Size of House :   Type of family :

No. of members in the household : Adults -
Children -

Occupation of other members :

Income from all sources :

I. **Educational Background and Aspirations**

A. If subject not attending school/college

a) What was the reason for your not attending school? OR
Why did you leave school ?

b) If you were not stopped from going to school would you have liked studying ? If yes, upto what class ?

c) In your view what are the advantages of education ?

d) Is formal education as essential for girls as it is for boys?

e) Do you supplement the family income in any way ?

f) If a girl is employed outside the home does her prestige

i) go up
ii) go down
iii) remain unchanged ?

g) Is formal education of the girl likely to improve her chances of making a 'good' marriage ?

h) What is your most earnest wish related to your own future ?

B. If subject attending an educational institution

a) In your view what are the advantages of formal education ?
b) Is formal education as essential for girls as it is for boys ?
c) For which of the following reasons do you go to school/college

i) Parents' wish
ii) You want to get education
iii) At this age it seems to be the right thing to do
iv) So that one does not have to sit idle at home
v) Education improve chances of making a 'good' marriage.

d) Do you wish to work after completing your education?

e) If a girl finds employment after completing her education does her prestige

a) go up
b) go down
c) remain unchanged ?

f) If no one stops you, upto what level would you like to study ? What do you want to do in life ?

g) What is your most earnest wish related to your own future ?

II. Socialisation

1. From your childhood onwards what differences have you observed in your brother's upbringing and yours ?

2. Have you observed differences in the upbringing of boys and girls ?

3. Do parents give greater freedom to boys as compared to girls ?

4. Why do you think greater significance is attached to a boy's birth as compared to a girl's birth ?

5. If someone asked you whether you wished to be a boy or a girl in your "next birth", what would be your answer?

6. Are you happy or unhappy that you are a girl ?

7. Among the siblings who does maximum work at home ?
8. (If subject does) do you do more work than others because you are a girl or you are the eldest or other siblings are boys ?

9. (If not) Why do you think you do not have to do much work in the house ?

10. Have you ever felt that because you are a female you have to attend to some jobs at home even if you do not wish to do so?

11. If your brother/sister refuses to do a job assigned to him/her what is your parent's reaction ?

12. Do you feel that as compared with your brother (or other males) there are more restriction on you ?

13. i) Do your parents keep a check on who your friends are ?
    ii) Have they ever objected to your friendship with a particular girl ?
    iii) Are you allowed to spend a night at your friend's house ?

iv) Are you allowed to go to your friend's house ?
v) If you go to visit a friend do you have to come back within a fixed time ?
vi) Are you permitted to go to the market and/or cinema with your friends ?

14. Are there any restriction on the kind of clothes you should not wear ?

15. Are you allowed to go out alone ?
Where ?
Upto what time ?

16. Are you satisfied with your place in the family, responsibilities assigned to you and the circumstances of your family ?

17. What do your parents generally emphasize with regard to your code of conduct ?

III. Menarche

1. At what age did you begin menstruation ?

2. Did you have any knowledge in this regard before you had this experience ?

3. What was your experience when you first menstruated ?

4. (If no prior knowledge) Do you feel that if you had been told about this change, it would have been better ? Who should have talked to you?

5. Why do you think this change occurs among girls and what is its' significance for the girl ?

6. Do you have to observe any restriction in the house during your menstruation period?

7. Around menarche did you feel a change in yourself, physically and emotionally ?

8. Did you experience any change in your willingness to work ?

9. Did you feel that around menarche there was an increase in parental restriction on your movements and activities ?

IV. Marriage

A. For Unmarried subjects

1 (i) In your opinion when will you be married off?

a) Within a year
b) Within 2 years
c) More than 2 years
d) Has no idea

(ii) Will your parents consult you before fixing your marriage?

2. Will you be prepared to get married whenever your parents find a suitable match for you ?

3. Have you ever talked to anyone in the family about the kind of person you would like to marry and when your marriage should take place ?

4. Have you ever thought about it ?

5. Do you have faith in your parents ' choice of a life partner for you ?

6. If for some reason you do not like the person your parents have selected for you will you talk to your parents about this ?

7. (If yes) If your parents rule out your objection and decide to go ahead with the marriage will you reconcile or retaliate ?

8. The amount of control that you think you can exercise over the selection of your life partner is
   a) Nil b) a little c) substantial

9. If you considered a person suitable to you for marriage and he belonged to your caste and community
   a) Will you convey it to your parents through someone else - like a friend or relation ?
   b) Will you speak directly to your parents ?
   c) Do you feel that you cannot dare to speak about it to your parents.

10. a) After marriage is it better to live with your in-laws or to be on your own ?

    b) Whose responsibility is it that conflicts do not arise between the two generations when living together - mother-in-law's or daughter-in-law's ?

    c) If there is constant conflict when living together is it wise to live separately or one of the two should compromise ?

B. For married subjects

1. a) For how long have you been married?

   b) When did your engagement take place ?

2. In your opinion did your marriage take place -
   a) at the right age ?
   b) before time ?
   c) late in life ?

3. Who selected your husband as your partner ?

4. a) Were you consulted before your marriage was fixed ?
   b) (If no) Do you feel that you should have been consulted before any decision was taken ?

5. Did you ever meet your husband before you were married ?
If yes a) Just saw him.
b) Met him in others' presence.
c) Met him alone.

6. Are you happy that you have married the right person ?

7. Before you were married, did you look forward to marriage or did you want it to be delayed as much as possible ?

8. Are you satisfied with the change in your life-style after marriage ?

9. How do you spend your day ?

10. a) If living in joint family - Do you prefer living the way you are living or do you think living independently would be better ?
b) If living independently - Do you like living independently or would you like to live with your in-laws ?

C For those betrothed to be married

1. a) How long ago were you engaged ?
b) Who selected the prospective bridegroom ?

2. a) Were you consulted before your marriage was fixed ?
b) (If no) Do you feel that you should have been consulted before any decision was taken ?

3. In your opinion, has your engagement taken place at the right age or early or late in life ?

4. Have you ever met your fiance ?

5. Are you satisfied that you are engaged to the right person ?

6. When will the marriage take place ?

7. Whenever your parents or future in-laws want, will you be prepared for marriage ?

8. a) After marriage should the couple continue to live in the joint family or live independently ?
   b) Between the mother-in-law and the daughter-in-law who has greater responsibility in maintaining cordial relations within the family ?
   c) If conflicts arise between the two generations, is it still important to live together or is it better to live separately then ?

Questions for all subjects

1. Should a girl be consulted before her marriage is fixed ?

2. In your opinion is there more freedom before marriage or after marriage ?

3. Is it necessary that every girl should get married ? Why ?

Index